MW01194923

Magical

BREADCRUMBS

Revealing the Path to Destiny

D'ANN MARIE BLATT

First published by Ultimate World Publishing 2023
Copyright © 2023 D'Ann Marie Blatt

ISBN

Paperback: 978-1-922982-90-2
Ebook: 978-1-922982-91-9

Cover design: Ultimate World Publishing
Layout and typesetting: Ultimate World Publishing
Editor: Vanessa McKay

Ultimate World Publishing
Diamond Creek,
Victoria Australia 3089
www.writeabook.com.au

Dedication

This book is dedicated to all those in the highest vibration within my soul society. I am eternally grateful for my spirit guides, angels, loved ones who have crossed, all those that have led me to where I am, and those in my life today.

To my husband, you have provided beyond measurable support through my journey of self-discovery and writing this book. I recognize my journey is difficult for you, and I thank you. I love you, and I'm just a little crazy!

To my mother, your love and support throughout my life have meant the world to me. I am here to show you the way to peace and joy. Just worry less, pray more, and believe in the magic of angels and the Universe!

To my Twin Flame, thank you for lighting my soul on fire! I am forever your little fireball and I'll love you throughout infinity and far beyond.

Contents

Foreword

Dear reader,

Imagine if there were a guidebook to life; A series of hacks that would make life easier, limit frustrations, increase your happiness, and potentially save time and money. Well, there is! They have been there all along, just waiting for you to discover them. All you need to do is open your heart and mind to possibilities. Anyone and everyone can tap into their guidebook by simply believing in what cannot be seen but only felt.

My words are intended to resonate within your heart; I have included a glossary to assist you in comprehending some of the content and concepts that may not yet be familiar to you but must be understood from the author's perspective. Please take a moment to review them before proceeding and refer to them as you need.

I have included sections for your reflection on the content throughout the book. Use these moments to apply your personal connections. Then take a break from reading to allow the information to be processed. It is likely that you will not immediately feel connected to the content. Keep pushing forward and allow yourself to recognize the deceptions and distractions preventing you from connecting.

Consider that some of the content may elicit highly emotional responses, referred to in society as triggering. Pay close attention to those times and the emotions that arise within you. These are keys to uncovering the shadows within you that are standing in your way of receiving. The last few pages of this book have been dedicated for you to jot down your feelings each time this happens. Recognizing patterns is also essential to unlocking your guidebook.

Magical Breadcrumbs is not only about you. Through our courageousness to embark on this journey of uncovering our authentic selves, we unite and transform as one. Our unity changes the world through more love, greater acceptance, and sovereignty of the collective. Can you imagine what an amazing place this world would be with more love, respect, and peace?

Before we go any further, prepare a refreshing beverage and find a comfortable place to allow yourself to go within to continue reading. Note that I will interchange terms to address Divine guidance throughout the book, but please insert the term you feel most comfortable with.

Source, Spirit, Universe, Divine, God or Higher Self,

Please open my heart and allow me to hear the messages and beauty of your work that D'Ann is sharing and provide calmness within myself to recognize my unlimited potential, and Magical Breadcrumbs.

Namaste

Disclaimer

I wrote this book from my heart. Everything within these pages comes from my experiences, interpretations, and beliefs. Although I have spent countless hours researching and reading, hoping to find concrete proof and evidence, very little exists. What I uncovered was an entire community that shares similar views and experiences. While some ideas are supported by science and the Bible, others are supported by an infinite possibility that something exists because you believe.

Prologue

Once upon a time, a long time ago, in a far, far away place, there was an enormous flash of light in the darkness. Source had created a new soul in the essence of its perfection to shine brightly and be one with the Universe for eternity. Each soul is a distinctive spark of light, stunning and complete with a dash of uniqueness and brilliance to share with the world.

In silence, the clouds rolled, and lightning flashed around them while Source held this new soul in its hands, in awe of yet another new creation to join all those it had made before. The soul appeared as a ball of sparkling light, pure energy moving and shaking, the excitement building within. But it was not quite ready yet.

With a thunderous voice, Source said, "Now, my little spark, you are perfect and free to roam anywhere you choose; I have made you to grow, learn, feel, and evolve while building relationships with many along the way. Your purpose is to spread my love, and all that is true, good, and beautiful everywhere you go."

Spark's excitement grew, and its light began bouncing with anticipation.

"But my little spark, if you choose to accept a mission on planet Earth to experience human life, you will encounter a force called ego that also lives invisibly inside every human you will meet. Their egos will attempt to dim your light. You must never let this happen. Instead, let your light change the human and make the world better. Inside you are all you will ever need, including hidden gifts that transcend the human experience. Use them to guide you. Oh, and my little spark, you are never alone. I and all the other sparks will support you, cheer you on, and show you the way to go with our Magical Breadcrumbs, and when you are finished, you will return to me as you are an eternal soul."

Bells began ringing softly in the distance. The time to fly drew near, and Source lowered its tone. "Never give up my little spark, even when you encounter conflict and challenges. Rest assured; they are all part of my divine plan for you to rise as an Earth Angel."

The bells became louder. The time had come to release little spark. Source sprinkles fairy dust on top, opens its hands, and blows a breath of wind, sending little spark sailing off, tumbling, like a dandelion in the wind. And as little spark picks up speed and begins to zip off, it hears Source's final words, "Just let love lead the way!"

Inside you is that spark, and you have chosen the mission to incarnate into a human on Planet Earth!

Chapter 1

Limited Perception

Never, in a million years, did I imagine that after half of my lifetime had passed, I would be starting anew. I find myself having recently graduated college, discovering my purpose, and writing this book; things that were only passing thoughts not so long ago. But if my life can take such an unexpected change, then so can yours.

Looking back, there was nothing exceptional about my early years. Honestly, on reflection, I see my childhood as a little boring. As a young child, I was always one of the smallest children in class, and often teased by the boys in school. I earned average grades and avoided extracurricular activities, as socializing never appealed to me. I developed only one true, long-lasting friendship, as I never felt like

I belonged. I was naturally responsible, mature, helpful, sensible, and empathetic toward others. Teachers loved me, and many referred to me as an 'old soul.'

My childhood home was stable and harmonious, although we moved frequently. As the youngest of four children and the only girl, I was most comfortable spending time with adults and observing others. I was likable because my personality was calm and easy-going. Religion was not apparent in the house, despite my grandfather being a Southern Baptist Minister. Sometimes, we went to services at church and said a prayer before dinner, but I always saw my great-grandmother get on her knees, fold her hands, and bow her head to pray before bedtime. My mom was my best friend, and I was happiest hanging out with her or spending time alone.

As an adult, I considered myself average. To an outside eye, I am 5' tall, 122 pounds, with brown hair and gray eyes. I avoided photographs because I have never seen a picture of myself that I did not immediately find something to criticize. Other women often misjudged me as arrogant, and I didn't understand the attention I attracted when walking into any room.

I am a mother to two teenage boys and a wife of over 25 years. I have been a business professional and community youth leader. I pride myself on having integrity and being trustworthy and dependable. I am caring, compassionate, reliable, efficient, fair, and professional. Supporting the success and growth of those I care about is important to me, and I love to lend a hand when someone asks. None of which I find outstanding; it is just getting harder to find people with these characteristics.

My identity was based on my family and work, and I was wrapped up in the business of being someone and doing something. I was always going and doing, feeling like there was never enough time. I hadn't sat on the couch in months, and I'd chosen responsibilities over recreation. I thought being productive, accomplishing things, and doing for others was what I was supposed to do, that somehow putting everyone and everything else before me made me a better person.

It was important to me for others to see me and my family as perfect. Whatever that means. (We will explore the concept of perfection in a future chapter.) But, to the outside world, I thought I appeared to have a perfect life. A beautiful family, a loving husband, a great job, a nice car, and everything else that provided the illusion I had it all together. I feared people realizing my children, my husband, my marriage, my parenting, and every other facet of my life were not the illusion of perfection they seemed. My heart was in the right place, but just as those who judge me prematurely are so incredibly wrong, I was getting it all wrong.

I tell you these very personal details for you to relate to and recognize those like me. My ego obscured my ability to truly experience the beauty in this world and discover my soul's purpose. I was blind to all the amazing gifts the Universe surrounded me with because I was focusing on all the wrong things. My time and energy were wasted failing to establish connections with others, not living in every moment, and falling victim to societal programming and limiting beliefs. I was standing in my own way of joy and happiness until I met someone who changed my life and helped me shed the illusions. Now, there are signs of extraordinary everywhere I turn.

Before we go any further, I need to clarify I am human and I have made choices not everyone will agree with. Please attempt to see the beauty in my journey and forgo judgment.

Reflection Section

Pause and reflect on your view of yourself. Throughout life, one is constantly evolving because of influences. Positive or negative, those influences create beliefs we establish deep within our subconscious minds that dictate our choices and lead us into living lives created by all our decisions instead of our soul's true purpose.

Start by listing all the roles you play in this lifetime: parent, sibling, spouse, child, co-worker, employee, friend, partner, lover, etc. Then, allow yourself to reflect on each one and think about how they impact your day-to-day life. Be sure to consider both the actions that feel enjoyable and raise positive feelings, and those that feel like a duty, an obligation, or weigh heavily on you, raising negative emotions.

Those you indicated negatively represent some areas of the 'wrong things' standing in your way of seeing the beauty surrounding you, while those you enjoy and are naturally good at are leading you to your life's purpose.

_____

_____

_____

_____

_____

_____

_____

_____

_____

We are all remarkable, and we each bring unique gifts into the world. It is through authentic interactions with others that we truly live life; growing and evolving as intended by our creator.

Chapter 2

Powerful Pioneering

In the simplest of terms, life is about experiences and how we feel. To get the most from this journey, Source has provided us with the tools of people and emotions. From mild to intense, all the feelings that ensue from human interactions are essential and provide free and limitless opportunities for growth, learning, and soul expansion. Like an all-you-can-eat buffet, meet as many people as possible and partake in all the emotions that naturally arise. The feelings within each of us and that we elicit in others are the primary interconnection of our existence and the secret to our success.

People

People are an integral part of life. In fact, they are the key to our success. Our entire lives, we interact with people. People were created for companionship, support, and to help one another during this lifetime. Some even agreed to play an important role, to guide you before you were born. But as we age, too often, we become absorbed in ourselves, comfortable in our established lives and routines, and accepting of our perceived limitations. We fail to initiate new connections and foster building relationships with people we already know, denying ourselves the chance to grow and experience joy and happiness. We were not created to be this way.

Children are born as social beings. When they see other children playing, they are eager to join them. They will approach one another and ask others to play, or just run up to a group and pick up where they are in an organized activity. They even touch one another, as they are unaware of the concept of space adults insist upon. It is not until they understand judgment and perceived limitations that this free and natural action becomes controlled by fear. Although controlled, the desire and ability for these connections are still inside each of us.

I urge you to step outside your comfort zone, try new things, and allow yourself to be vulnerable and play. When you open yourself up to making connections, amazing things happen. Most of these interactions invoke gradual, subtle changes within that you hardly notice. However, others elicit instantaneous transformations that are hard to overlook. Surprising sources of joy and happiness exist in interactions and connections with others.

It all begins with realizing that meaningful connections are essential to living a fulfilling life. Through opening our closed mindsets and understanding we are all in this together and everyone equally matters, we dissolve the illusions that life is a competition or a race, and we can all win. Life is a journey we each meander through on our own paths, and our time on this planet does not dictate who or where we should be or what we should have accomplished. Everyone's journey is as unique as they are and should be celebrated.

Somewhere deep inside each of us are those children we once were. Make the child inside you proud by meeting and playing with new people. Some of those new connections just might surprise you with how much they change your life.

Profound Relationships

Throughout our lives, we are impacted by purposeful relationships for our growth and evolution. These are profound relationships divinely introduced into life through soul guidance, based on agreements made before this lifetime. Each one has a distinct purpose and brings unique possibilities for healing, experiencing life, and expanding one's soul.

Profound relationships span across labels and categories of identifiers that people place upon others. These relationships can be strictly familial, romantic, platonic, or a combination between them. They can span significant age gaps, varying races, or cross gender lines. The connection lies between the souls, and souls do not discriminate. An open mind is essential when meeting new people because one never knows when one might meet someone who holds the key to unlocking their potential. All profound relationships are Magical Breadcrumbs.

Soul Mates

Think about the relationships that seem purposeful to you, those you can see the significance in your life since knowing or meeting them. They may be currently in your life, or have come and gone, stayed for an extended period, arrived suddenly and disappeared, or popped in and out occasionally. Soulmates can appear at any point in life and in any role. Friends, family members, business partners, spouses, children, lovers, or even a casual acquaintance can be soulmates. Soulmates are typically naturally compatible, elicit feelings of familiarity, and are supportive and nurturing, easy-going, and comfortable; however, that is not always the case. Each one's purpose is to support the growth of the soul.

Soulmate relationships exist in this life because their souls agreed to take on different roles to support and accompany one another not only in this lifetime, but on many lifetime journeys and reunite between incarnations. They are part of a soul family, also known as a soul cluster, which are souls connected in eternity.

The concept of soulmate relationships is commonly accepted and believed to exist. However, our human minds and established beliefs typically relate soulmates to romantic relations. Soulmates are anyone who has significantly impacted your life, no matter how big or how small. If you remember the interaction or relationship and reflect on the time spent with them, it was likely a soulmate encounter.

Personal Soulmate Connection

People I recognize thus far in my life who are souls that agreed to help me on my journey:

- Best friends for over forty years. Although she is not related by blood, she is my sister. She explicitly recalls the Magical Breadcrumbs when she saw me in elementary school and felt a connection and strong desire to become friends. We have been able to rely on one another throughout our lives through ongoing support, acceptance, and love. Some of the best therapy is in the form of matching pajamas, and a weekend getaway where we laugh until we cry, just like we did as young girls. Although separated by distance, when we unite, it's like we never parted.

- My husband for over half of my life. Although almost complete opposites, he is my stability and comfort. I can count on him for support and alternative perspectives; even if I don't like what he says, we always find common ground in acceptance.

- An unlikely middle school friendship rekindled 30 years later when she briefly resurfaced in my life and provided the confidence and emotional support at the most opportune time to be the catalyst for my career change and alignment with certain people and places toward my destiny.

- A friendship after high school that developed spontaneously and only lasted for a few months but provided the opportunity to place us both on our paths to meet our spouses.

- A new friend that shares similar spiritual beliefs. Joined together through an online meetup group, helping one another grow and serve the purposes of our souls.

- An employee I hired who only stayed a few months. She provided relief and the ability for me to focus on my health and family. A Christmas card depicting a baby in a manger foretold the miracle I would receive that Christmas morning.

- A casual acquaintance working together at our children's school opened the door for me to align with a new career opportunity and the timing to meet my Twin Flame.

Reflection Section

Pause and reflect on those in your life now or previously that you consider to be one of your soul mates. What is it about the relationship that led you to believe they were a soulmate? Were there profound changes in your life you link to this person, or is it more of unexplained feelings of comfort or purpose?

_____

_____

_____

_____

_____

_____

You just never know who is here to play such an instrumental role in your soul's journey. Sometimes, it is only for a moment; other times, they are here forever; soulmates are some of the greatest gifts in this lifetime.

Karmic

Envision relationships that cause more pain than pleasure. More turbulence than calmness. A relationship that feels as if it ends, only to begin again. You return to them out of a glimpse of possibilities, or you attract subsequent situations with the same issues. These are the most volatile of profound relationships; they are karmic.

Although undefined by dictionaries, it is commonly accepted that the purpose of a karmic relationship is to teach valuable lessons and heal karmic debts. Although karma can bring both positive and negative energies, these relationships surface to provide golden opportunities to resolve past wrongdoings, make choices in alignment with what is good and right, and learn from one's previous mistakes. The resurfaced patterns will continue to rise until the attached karma is healed. Those who cannot recognize the patterns often refer to it as bad luck or being cursed.

These relationships are painful, emotionally exhausting, and usually short in duration but serve essential purposes in one's healing and growth. At first you are drawn to them, but then they feel irritating and uncomfortable. They raise issues and hit hot spots within you, causing you to want to run away, but you feel pulled to them repeatedly. The good times are high, and the bad times are really low, leaving one feeling exhausted from the seemingly never-ending rollercoaster ride. Some kind of drama is always arising in a karmic relationship.

There are harmful tendencies to control or be controlled, and jealousy, abuse, and codependency are common indicators of a karmic relationship. You ask yourself why you are in this relationship but have trouble letting go. Karmic relationships easily and quickly become toxic and harmful and never end well.

Personal Karmic Connection

My first karmic relationship was with a boyfriend in my teenage years. He could be the nicest, most loving guy and then the meanest and most hateful. He was controlling and emotionally, sexually, and physically abusive, and I was co-dependent. I thought I could help him or somehow save him. Thankfully, separation with relocation and incarceration ended this toxicity. Following, I attended counseling and learned about the concepts and indicators of co-dependency, which prepared me for the next encounter that raised the same dysfunctional patterns. I recognized the signs, saw the similarities, and chose not to continue the relationship, thus healing the karma associated and stopping the lessons from repeating.

Pause and reflect on a relationship in your past that feels like it was likely karmic. Can you identify additional relationships that had similar patterns? Did you learn anything from the connection about yourself? If you think you are still in the karmic cycle, what are the repeating signs, and what do you need to heal to stop the pattern from returning?

_____

_____

_____

_____

_____

_____

_____

_____

Realize that you are a powerful, sovereign being, never a victim. It is not what happens to you, but how you react that determines the future. Holding onto the victim mentality of poor me, not accepting responsibility for your actions, and doing nothing to improve yourself ensures the likelihood of repeating. It is when one learns from the situation and makes different choices that the pattern is disrupted, and karma is transmuted.

Twin Flames

**One's life will never be the same
after meeting their Twin Flame.**

Imagine for a moment what your life would be like if you met someone who shared your values, desires, and dreams. Someone who made you feel at ease, your chemistry just clicked with, who magnetically attracted you, and who showed you how to become the best version of yourself. Someone who accepted and loved you unconditionally and wanted nothing more than for you to be happy and entirely your authentic self. Sounds amazing, right? That is a Twin Flame, also known as a Mirror Soul.

Although the concept of Twin Flames and Mirror Souls is less known and accepted by people than soulmates, the concept can be traced as far back as 360 B.C.E. in the philosophical text, *Symposium* by the ancient philosopher, Plato, and supported within the Bible book of Genesis; however, there has been no scientific evidence yet discovered to support the theory. But for those who have experienced this profound connection that touches the depths of one's heart and soul, there is no denying it. It changes one's life and opens one's mind to realities of telepathy, extrasensory perception, epiphanies, astral travel, and one's heart to unconditional love and acceptance revealed within and between Twin Flames that spreads to other close relationships and the world around them.

A Twin Flame is a mirror of you, and everyone has one somewhere in the Universe. They are souls connected for all eternity, created of the same energetic blueprint. It is the Ying to the Yang. When united in flesh, Twin Flames ignite an intense experience of personal transformation. All one's strengths and weaknesses are reflected, and each is forced to see all their fears, insecurities, and traumas through profound lessons, helping them individually reach their highest potential and find balance internally of their feminine and masculine energies. The phases of the Twin Flame journey bring feelings of being a blessing and a curse.

The purpose of the journey of Twin Flames is to bring consciousness and growth to each other, pushing them to set aside their egos and reach their soul contracts. It is not only a personal journey of self-transformation to return both souls to their pure, authentic selves and align with their highest potential and Source, but to show others what unconditional love looks like and to spread the concept that love should be free and liberated.

The journey of Mirror Souls is difficult. It includes recognizing illusions and facing and healing false egoic beliefs, and karma. It is a grueling feat for those who have developed strong egos and have fallen prey to societal programming, resulting in the desire to run or control circumstances from the intensity. But, this relationship does not operate on the same levels as other human relationships. Attempting to control, manipulate, or deny the growth and personal changes only results in separation, frustration, and perpetuation of the cycle.

One must accept there is no turning back to how you used to be before meeting your Mirror Soul. One does not get over a Twin Flame or just move on with their life like they did after previous relationships. Their Twin Flame is their beloved, and they hold a divine connection not only to the hearts and souls of one another, but to Source.

Although permanent physical unions are possible, they are uncommon, but the soul union can never be broken. When separated, each soul continues to search for the connection, through an echolocation between the heart chakras of both twins, resulting in intense longing and yearning, feeling like torture and punishment. It is then that they must face and heal the surfaced wounds or spend the rest of their lives trying to hide them or drown in self-destructive behavior. Once healed, they can surrender to each other, unite in oneness, combine their soul gifts, and rise together to fulfill the final purpose of the union.

It is also important to note a Twin Flame connection exists between souls and that the connection is not restricted by societal beliefs, limitations, or cultural norms. Twin Flames can be within those of the same or different sex, race, or religion and age and geographic separations are common.

Personal Twin Flame Connection

There are over eight billion people on the planet, and I was fortunate enough to meet my Twin Flame in this lifetime. With those odds, it is easy to see that it is nothing short of a divinely orchestrated miracle. If you are like me, before reading this chapter, you may have never heard the term Twin Flame, or maybe you associated it with a soulmate. Although both are profound relationships that stem from the connection of souls, meeting soulmates are common, while encountering one's Twin Flame is rare.

One single person in this world changed my entire life. He was the catalyst for my spiritual awakening. From day one, I could feel changes happening within me, but it wasn't until years later, when a psychic explained our connection, that I began to understand and learn about this phenomenon. Through my recount of our relationship, I hope you comprehend the depths of this induced transformation that led you to hold this book in your hands. My Twin Flame encounter is a beautiful gift I am thankful for, regardless of the pain. Magical Breadcrumbs brought us together, and Magical Breadcrumbs keep us apart.

Glimpse

The first glimpse of my Twin Flame occurred in a business meeting, and I couldn't shake the surge of energy that ignited within me. For days, I dismissed the feelings as excitement for an incredible professional opportunity. But from the moment I met this stranger, it was obvious that the strong sense of connection felt different from any other I'd ever experienced. There was an unexplainable comfort like we had known each other forever, an undeniable attraction, and when our eyes met, it was intoxicating. Every time we were together, the Magical Breadcrumbs led us to continue exploring our connection, and we were eager to follow them.

For over a year, we worked together and developed a friendship and respect for one another. We kept our interactions professional, but inside each of us, things were changing. Without us realizing, our soul connection began aligning us with our authentic selves. Each of us began to drop old bad habits, look at aspects of our lives where we weren't meeting our potential, and the focus turned to enjoying life and having experiences that made us feel alive. Unbeknownst to us, the purpose of the Twin Flame connection was hard at work. We were addicted to one another's energy because it was identical.

Life Changing Decision

After our professional affiliation ended, we pursued the desire that had been burning between us for far too long. Although I am not proud of the decision to break my vows, I knew I would regret it for the rest of my life if I didn't. I wanted nothing more than to finally feel his touch. It was an intense, innate attraction and desire, a magnetic pull drawing him to me.

It was within those first moments of intimacy our souls recognized one another. As the pieces of the puzzle were put together, our energies combined to create a force of unconditional love accompanied by an ability to see into the window of one another's soul. It was when we lowered our ego defenses that there was a recognition and remembrance of our soul's unity. The intensity blindsided both of us and left us bewildered and thirsty for an understanding of what was happening.

A lifetime of human-based relationship experiences and emotions were torn to shreds, and our true selves were revealed. I still cannot express the strength and power of this connection. But whatever it was, we knew three things: One, this was not normal. Neither of us had ever experienced anything even remotely close. Two, it could not be dismissed or disregarded. It had really happened. Three, this was not the ending, but a beautiful new beginning. There was no turning back. The more time we spent together, the more Magical Breadcrumbs materialized.

The Fairy-Tale

What ensued after those first moments of intimacy can only be described as free, limitless, completely natural, and the purest form of beauty, joy, and love. The second purpose of the Twin Flame journey was beginning for me. I was remembering my connection to Source. I began praying regularly, including a prayer that my husband would find it within his heart to understand my indiscretions. A blessing that later came true that I can only accredit God for making a reality. I was willing to risk everything for the feelings and changes that our time together elicited inside me.

With him, my actions and words were effortless and spontaneous; they were in alignment with my soul. I broached unusual relationship topics of conversation like vulnerability and avoiding resisting what felt so natural. Strange physical changes began happening like the tingle in my lower spine, a feeling of weight lifted from my shoulders, and I started experiencing what I call 'soul explosions.' Where the body, heart, mind, and soul are in alignment, resulting in utter ecstasy. A soul explosion encompasses one's entirety and returns one momentarily to the purity of the soul, resulting in visions of infinite blackness and stars swirling and leaving you in a blissful state. It is an orgasm multiplied by at least a thousand times. I became obsessed with the possibility of experiencing this euphoria every time we united.

Magic Eyes

Our eyes began seeing through the lens of our souls. I apply the old phrase, 'love is blind' used by Shakespeare and Chaucer, to the vision through a Twin Flames' eyes. Twins possess 'magic eyes,' revealing perfection and light within everything first. They elicit feelings of unconditional love and complete acceptance. Magic eyes appear dilated and shine twinkles of light reflecting the infinite Universe. It's a temporary blinding of all things that truly do not matter, those that are connected to the ego and not the soul.

My twin's ability to see me through his magic eyes bypassed my physical insecurities and allowed me to love every part of me. I no longer looked into the mirror and saw all my imperfections, but my feminine image created in perfection. I felt grateful for what my body has done in this lifetime. I saw the scars and wrinkles as evidence of decades spent experiencing life and a remembrance of my journey to be celebrated, not ashamed, like society leads you to believe.

My magic eyes allowed me to see his magnificent yellow aura. Literally radiant and virtually glowing; a yellow light illuminating him, like an actor under stage lights. Validation he was joyful, happy, and confident, and his solar plexus chakra flowed freely. I saw unconditional love, acceptance, and desire before the choices of his ego life.

The gift of my magic eyes has remained, allowing me to see the allure in others and situations. Life before opening my magic eyes appeared muted and out of focus. Now I see clearly. I see the vast array of colors in the world as more vibrant and vivid, with all the shades from a giant box of Crayola crayons surrounding me everywhere I look. I hope I never lose this vision. It allows me to see the beauty, goodness, and potential in the world before anything else.

The Bubble Phase

All of this occurred in the beginning of our Twin Flame relationship, commonly referred to as the bubble phase. So, to say, it is the carrot that leads the horse. It is a love story Hollywood and Disney attempt to portray in movies and fairytales. This is the Universe's way of showing the twins the heaven on Earth that will be experienced if they can surrender and continue to follow the Magical Breadcrumbs.

But all bubbles pop eventually, uncovering the true purpose of this union. The Twin Flame journey is not about a love story. Sure, it's the ego's reward for supporting the soul's journey if one can survive the evolution of self, but it is not the purpose. Through the ego's interference and attempt to control the relationship, wounds surface within each twin that must be healed to continue. This causes periods of separation and the eruption of toxic or turbulent times between them.

Our bubble phase lasted for years. Until the reality of this lifetime came crashing in. My husband confronted me about the affair, and my marriage, family, and ego life, as I knew it, went into turmoil and transformation. My Twin Flame ran from me to protect his ego and materialistic life, and I fell into a dark night of the soul. It may sound like chaos, and I assure you it was, but it was divine timing for the next phase of my soul's evolution, and the words of my twin carried me through the darkest time of my life:

"Never, not for a minute, do I not love you."
My Twin Flame

The Dark Night of the Soul

The dark night of the soul may also be a new concept to you. The best way to describe this excruciating pain is numbness. It feels like a separation of the soul from the ego. My soul took control of my physical body, and I became only an observer.

Uncontrollable tears fell from my eyes. My mind was completely clear of all thoughts. My hearing was muted, and obstructed by faint, distant white noise. My body parts felt incredibly heavy and nearly impossible to move. My vision was hazy and my breathing was very shallow. Hunger and thirst were non-existent. To an outsider, it could be misdiagnosed as severe depression, or that death was inevitable. This stage lasted for days. I was unaware of the day, the date, or the time. However, it felt like it was all I had ever known. That is until I began to awaken.

As I lay on the couch, I suddenly became aware of a beam of sunshine on my face, and I received a clear, clairaudient message I'll share with you in a future chapter. As I opened my eyes, I felt renewed and had an overwhelming sense of a new beginning. I felt a sense of purpose and excitement for the future. I felt comforted and loved. I longed for my twin, but it was clear this part of the journey was for me to walk alone. It was within the first steps of the path that I began to see myself as an image of perfection in the only eyes that mattered, and I realized it all had purpose.

Changed Forever

My Twin Flame set my soul on fire!

My life will never be the same. Undoubtedly, my Twin Flame set my soul on fire and regardless of the egoic decisions we made to be apart, I vowed to continue to heal myself and build my relationship with Source, to shine my light brightly and share our love with the world. Whether physically together or apart, he remains an essential part of my life as a best friend, a teacher, a healer, and an ultimate lover. I find comfort in knowing time does not exist between souls, and reuniting is as if we never parted. In this lifetime, I hold a safe space for him if he chooses to follow my lead to heal and remember his connection with Source, and I anxiously await seeing if we fulfill our mission together. And if not, I'm tucked in his heart and holding his hand, and perhaps we'll choose to try again in another lifetime. But one thing is certain; the love and passion we shared in this life is etched into our souls for all eternity.

Reflection Section

Pause and reflect on the miracle of Twin Flames. Although the hopeful romantic in each of us may think this connection is the perfect partner we have been looking for, this type of relationship transcends everything that we, as people, think we know about love and relationships. Yet it unlocks passion, the deepest of all emotions within oneself; passion for one another, passion for life, and passion for living.

Disguised as the greatest love story of my life, is the lesson that one's life can change dramatically by meeting a single person. Can you identify someone now or in the past that you accredit to changing your life? Recognize that the relationship you identify could have positively or negatively impacted your life. How has your life changed?

_____

_____

_____

_____

_____

_____

_____

_____

_____

Although finding my Twin Flame was part of my path, I believe anyone can experience the benefits. When one has an open heart and mind and opens themselves to new people, experiences, and emotions, Magical Breadcrumbs appear, and miracles happen!

Chapter 3

Emerging Emotions

Emotions. Everyone encounters them. Some people have been programmed to be open and accepting of them, welcoming each one; while others learned to suppress, dismiss, ignore, and deny them. Emotions range from mild to intense and low to high. Lasting a moment or staying too long. Emotions are made of energy and are complicated, but all have a purpose.

Emotions are a compass pointing the way our souls need to go. The highs and lows, the good and the bad; it is experiences that bring the spectrum of emotions we are subjected to from the beginning until the end of our lives. Although it may not always feel like it, our emotions are leading us in the right direction. Those considered high like happiness, joy, and excitement are easy to see, but those disguised as low, such as fear, anger, and sadness, may be obscured. Each one's arising is showing you an area that requires your attention to heal, to learn, or to evolve.

The people we meet throughout our lives bring us experiences that engage our five senses of seeing, touching, hearing, tasting, and smelling, which ignite emotions. Through the embracing of occasions and the feelings they raise, we must allow them to naturally unfold and absorb as much as we can, while remembering that they are only energy passing through us. Sometimes this isn't easy because of the way we have been taught to handle our emotions.

You likely need to change your perspective on emotions. As young children, we are shown and taught how to handle emotions by those surrounding us. Many times, the adults that hold such influential power perpetuate the cycle of how they were raised, while incorporating their beliefs and experiences. Unfortunately, this results in the mentality that the experience raising the emotion is more important than the emotions that arise, that life goes on and one should get over it. Yes, every experience, both the good and the bad, is all part of life. But, the way they make you feel is where the importance lies.

Using the acronym FEEL will help you through the life cycle of emotions:

- **F-** Feel as the emotions arise naturally. Look at them as opportunities and understand that suppressing, ignoring, and avoiding them does not eliminate them. The goal here is to keep the energy flowing through you.

- **E**- Everything is purposeful; the people and the experiences leading to the emotional responses, the emotions that arise and how they make you feel. They are all part of your journey.

- **E**- Equally acknowledge all emotions. Do not dismiss or deny the arising because they are unpleasant, unwelcomed by others, or inconvenient.

- **L**- Let them go. Honoring the experiences, both good and bad, and their impact on you is the purpose. Sometimes this can be done alone; other times support and help from loved ones, friends, and mental health professionals are necessary.

You are entitled to feel any way you choose. The influence or presence of others should not constrict or dictate your emotional responses. Each of us feels circumstances differently. That does not make it wrong or bad, just simply different and should not be compared to others. This is especially important when dealing with children and young adults as they are impressionable and figuring out how to handle their arising.

High and Low Vibration Emotions

High vibrational emotions make you feel good. The associated energy is light, moves easily, is welcomed and is generally not denied and, therefore, moves through the body quickly and is released. These can often be seen in smiles and heard in laughter. Those experiencing high vibrational emotions have tendencies leaning toward communicating positively, accepting, uplifting, and working with others. The higher the vibration, the closer to one's personal truth and soul alignment.

Examples of high vibration emotions include but are not limited to: peace, love, joy, happiness, hope, admiration, optimism, trust, freedom, pleasure, elation, courageousness, bravery, contentment, excitement, satisfaction, resonance, and approval.

Low vibrational emotions are unpleasant, heavier, and move slowly. They get stuck in your body because one tries not to feel the pain they often bring; leading to physical manifestations of ailments resulting from old emotions you failed to honor and release. Tendencies of those experiencing low vibration emotions are judgment, comparing, competing, critiquing, and criticizing others. Those in lower vibrational patterns often unknowingly relinquish personal power, as they are more easily controlled and manipulated.

Examples of low vibration emotions include but are not limited to: fear, jealousy, sadness, anger, embarrassment, insecurity, worry, submission, doubt, resentment, disappointment, grief, hurt, pity, irritation, abandonment, aggressiveness, pessimism, disgust, control, overwhelmed, threatened, concerned, shame, depression, remorse, and hate.

Both high and low vibrational energies are Magical Breadcrumbs. But there are three emotions that are distinctly divine gifts that deserve a closer look: excitement, intuition, and resonance.

There's Magic Already Inside You

We are all born with some innate Magical Breadcrumbs. These are the divine gifts that transcend the human experience. Think of them as a comparison between applications pre-loaded into your cellular telephone by the manufacturer.

The apps operate stealthily in the background, virtually undetected making the smart device function, just like gifts from Source. These innate Magical Breadcrumbs arise through experiencing the five senses when life happens naturally. How we feel is the essence of our existence.

Excitement

Do you know the feeling you get in your body when something sparks your enthusiasm? Emotions arise from eagerness and anticipation, making it difficult to think about anything else. When intense enough, the situations can temporarily consume you, and you daydream about future possibilities. The feeling is excitement, and it is a divine gift.

Excitement flows freely in children. Children do not control their emotions; simple things like a trip to the park or Grandma's visit elicit excitement. They openly show this excitement in their actions. They jump around and smile and shout words of expression of how they are feeling. It's not until adults begin telling them to calm down, stop, or be quiet that they learn the feeling is something bad and unwelcome, and they begin to manipulate what flows so naturally.

The adults unknowingly alter the attunement of the child's divine gift of excitement through their ingrained beliefs and perceived limitations. Children who grow up in nurturing environments with patient, aware, and selfless influences learn how to recognize and express those moments, honoring and building upon their gift. While children who are exposed to controlling, detached, or selfish adults learn to fear it, fearing what the consequences will be for sharing, resulting in the beginning of the suppression and a detachment from a natural ability to recognize Magical Breadcrumbs.

As adults, we often try to control excitement and are not as in tune with this emotion when it arises. We may suppress the feeling from early childhood conditioning, or maybe we are too busy to allow ourselves to feel it, or we are afraid of the responses of others or fearful of what the excitement could lead to. The opportunities to receive this become fewer because we are preoccupied with life responsibilities (i.e., focusing on the wrong things). But they are still there!

The feelings of excitement are the Universe leading you somewhere. Magical Breadcrumbs disguised as excitement show you the way to your highest good and destiny. It's nearly impossible to determine the reason at the time, but they are designed to lead you to a person, place, or experience on your journey. Like bits of crackers thrown before a duck, the Universe wants you to continue to follow the path for more rewards.

Following excitement is like being on a treasure hunt using an invisible map to find riches of joy and happiness! But if you don't take the bait of excitement and follow the clues, the riches stay just outside your grasp, and you'll likely feel disappointment or regret. So, take a chance and allow yourself to experience the excitement. Joy and happiness are better than disappointment or regret any day. And all it takes is to say yes to the breadcrumbs of excitement!

Personal Connection to Excitement

When my youngest son was three, he was drawn to a pirate cartoon; a rarity for him, as he was not usually interested in what was on the television. He would practically burst with excitement when it came on. His eyes glued to the screen, he would sing the songs and mimic the motions of the main character. So, searching for treasure became our playtimes. We made maps and packed a treasure box with gold coins and gems. Then we would take turns hiding the treasures and leading one another on adventures through the house dressed in our eye patches and bandanas, looking through our telescopes, and warding off the bad guys with our swords until we found the treasure, laughing and smiling the entire time.

I intentionally fueled our special time together through his genuine interest by encouraging him to follow his excitement. He was building his imagination, learning to trust his instincts, developing leadership qualities, and increasing his verbal and motor skills while reinforcing our bond and having fun. But most importantly, I was planting seeds that having fun and following feelings of excitement are essential no matter how old one gets.

Reflection Section

Pause and reflect on the last time you felt excited. It may have been when presented with a new opportunity to go somewhere or do something or when you met someone new. How did you react? Did you follow the Magical Breadcrumb? How do you feel now, knowing it was a message from the Universe attempting to lead you toward your highest good?

_____

_____

_____

_____

_____

_____

_____

_____

_____

Following the feelings of excitement can also lead to passion, the most intense and desirable emotion. Passion is the ecstasy of all feelings. It is where the real magic lies! Passion has the power to alchemize and provide deeper personal fulfillment. It is the missing ingredient turning responsibility into living and loving into earth-shattering. Identify your passions, and you'll likely find a key to your life's purpose.

Gut Feelings

Do you know that intense feeling you get when you have a strong sense about someone or something? If you think about it, you can probably recall a time when you felt afraid but were unsure of why. Your emotional intelligence sensed dark energies and fear, and you received the gut feeling reinforcing the inner knowing to guide you away from the threat or danger. Although I used an example of keeping you from harm, this also happens for positive guidance. Later, I will share a personal story of having a gut feeling so strong I chased it for weeks, and it changed my life.

A gut feeling is a form of intuition. Each is defined as feelings or reactions based on instinctive feelings or emotional responses rather than conscious meaning. Both are Magical

Breadcrumbs! The Universe is steering you toward or away from certain people and circumstances to align you toward your highest good.

Learning to recognize, respect, and follow your gifts of intuition is vital to follow a path toward your destiny. There is no physical proof, and you cannot prove intuition. It is something your soul recognizes. Anyone can learn to tap into this ability and utilize it as a valuable tool to guide themselves. It is like using a compass to lead one in the right direction toward making the best decisions in life, both big and small.

When you quiet your ego mind, ask, and listen, you will feel what decision or direction you are being led toward. It is your own personal guidebook, your higher self. And the more you do it, the easier it becomes. However, often, the difficult part is not learning how to ask for guidance or hearing the answer; it is acting on the guidance received over what your egoic mind is telling you. It is inner knowing and trust in oneself that makes this practice become perfect.

Personal Connection to Gut Feeling

It was summertime in the early 90s. I had just graduated from high school and returned from a senior trip where I met a new friend with whom I had been in school for four years but had never known. For fun, we cruised the Las Vegas Strip; something kids our age did on weekends after the sun went down to socialize.

One Saturday night, with the windows down and the music up cruising, we pulled up to a traffic light, and in the lane beside us, I saw this mini truck with an attractive, dark-haired guy sitting in the bed looking my way. Our eyes met, and he said, "Smile." I flashed him a forced smile and silently hoped the light would change to escape this awkward moment. Eventually, we parted in traffic and returned to my friend's house for the night. I thought it was the end, but apparently, it was just the beginning.

He may have left my sight, but he did not leave my mind. Day and night, thoughts of him kept arising, and I knew I had to see him again. The week seemed to last forever, as I was so excited to go and find him. To my disappointment, he was nowhere to be seen. That night, I remember an overwhelming feeling of regret and disappointment. I felt like I had made a colossal mistake and had to find him. It took weeks of trying, but the feeling never waned.

Three weeks later, I spotted him and finally officially met him. He was everything I could have hoped for, and more. It felt like I had known him forever; being together was natural and comfortable, and we couldn't spend too much time together. But then, for some unknown reason, we started drifting apart, and life returned to what it was before we met. But fate had other plans; apparently, we were meant to be.

Reflection Section

Pause and reflect on the last time you had a gut feeling or sensed intuition. Were the feelings positive or negative? Did the feeling change your originally intended actions, or did you disregard it? Looking back, can you recognize the reason you had the feeling? How do you feel now, knowing it was a Magical Breadcrumb to guide or protect you?

_____

_____

_____

_____

_____

_____

_____

_____

Looking back, it is often easier to see the connection between how you felt and what happened and identify the unseen influences of Magical Breadcrumbs. Those were likely the times you were focusing on the right things, those happening right in front of you, referred to commonly as the 'now' moments. You were in flow with life without attempting to control anything.

Resonance

The innate ability of resonance is not as obvious as excitement and gut feelings, but it lies inside each of us. You have likely experienced resonance without realizing it when you heard or saw something that you immediately agreed with without questioning any further. For some unknown and unexplained reason, you accepted something as absolute when it was presented to you. But it does not always occur so effortlessly. This innate ability to recognize when something resonates within your inner being requires you to stop and feel the information you are taking in and then identify if the effect of the information appeals to you with some emotional significance.

Resonance is the realization of one's truth and is an important element in spiritual growth and recognizing Magical Breadcrumbs. Anyone can learn to tap into the space within the heart that connects information with emotions, providing the opportunity to evaluate received information. The key is allowing yourself to receive and evaluate without the interference of your ego, false beliefs, and logical thoughts and listening to your heart, and then accepting and holding onto what is in resonance and alignment with your personal truth and releasing what is not.

Information that is not in resonance should be let go, as it is not meant for you at this time. Sometimes resonance arrives instantaneously, and you don't notice the emergence in your life. While at other times, it starts as a feeling or thought that you cannot shake off in varying degrees, from barely noticeable to all-consuming. When you find yourself thinking about something after the moment has passed, the connection to resonance should be reconsidered and reevaluated, as on a higher level, you are being guided to it. It is essential to recognize resonance may change as one's life and soul evolves and that parts of the received information may resonate while others do not. Like the words in this book, many are likely resonating with you, while some may not entirely.

Personal Connection to Resonance

Years ago, I came across a transformational public speaker by the name of Kyle Cease. As I listened to his words, I remember thinking his message was far-fetched, and honestly, I did not understand all his ideas and concepts, but something about him spoke to a part of me I did not know existed yet. I had not even heard of resonance, but I recognized on some unexplainable level, I identified with his messages; they resonated within me, and I continued to listen to his words of wisdom.

I attribute Magical Breadcrumbs to Kyle's messages reaching me. I still do not know how I came across him online, but looking back, I can see that he was pivotal to finding my spiritual path and following my soul's purpose. In fact, My Magical Breadcrumb of hearing his message has led you to yours. Remember, people are instrumental in our journeys. We are all interconnected.

Reflection Section

Pause and reflect on the concept of resonance. Can you identify a time you felt an inner connection? Did you immediately accept the information as truth, or did it have to sit within your mind before reevaluating it with your heart? Ultimately, did you own it as part of your truth? How do you feel knowing that resonance is a Magical Breadcrumb guiding you?

Stop

Stop and think about all the people, the profound relationships, experiences, and emotions that you have been fortunate to have in this life. It is essential to recognize that the ability to connect with other people beyond just interacting is vital to our existence and through acts of kindness, acceptance, empathy, caring and compassion for others we make space for each to embrace our individuality and align with our purposes. It is when we are true to ourselves and make choices in life that fulfill our soul's needs that we are honoring our spark and aligning ourselves to receive Magical Breadcrumbs.

Chapter 4

Revolutionary Perspective

By definition, a breadcrumb is a tiny piece of dried bread. Often used in cooking, but more commonly known to be found on the bottom of a toaster or plate or lying on the kitchen counter. They are seemingly insignificant morsels of bread left behind that need to be wiped up and thrown away. However, a single breadcrumb has the potential to be so much more.

If you know the story of Hansel and Gretel, a classic fairy tale first published in 1812, you might remember that breadcrumbs were the last hope a young boy had of finding his way home. This story in children's literature, I remember hearing my mother read to me as a small child, has stuck with me throughout my life. While being led deep into the forest, Hansel tore bits of bread off a slice and dropped them along the trail, hoping to follow them home in the morning. Now, here I am, decades later, excited about the possibilities of breadcrumbs. If breadcrumbs could lead Hansel back in the direction he came from, breadcrumbs can surely lead one forward in a new direction toward something. All it would take is for someone to drop them and one to recognize them. And that's when it all clicked for me that the unseen guidance each of us receives are our own personal breadcrumbs, our Magical Breadcrumbs.

Magical Breadcrumbs: A morsel of wisdom in the form of a synchronicity or sign from the Universe attempting to lead one toward their highest good and ultimate destiny.

Magical Breadcrumbs are used by higher powers, including God, Spirit, Universe, Source, angels, spirit guides, and departed loved ones providing hints and clues to light the way for one to follow their soul's desires, accomplish lessons, and provide experiences within this life, ultimately leading one to reach their highest potential in this lifetime.

Magical Breadcrumbs appear throughout our lives. They are hidden gems in plain sight that appear when you pay attention to what is happening right before you and follow your intuition. It's about patterns and connections to meaningful symbols and words. Magical Breadcrumbs reinforce your thoughts or guide you toward a new idea, person, or situation.

The list of potential Magical Breadcrumbs is endless because they are crafted just for you. A song playing with lyrics of what you need to hear or what you were thinking about, repeating numerical patterns, thinking of someone, and then seeing or hearing from them, unexplainable recurring themed posts on social media, the arising of something meaningful to you and someone that has passed, gut feelings, and those of coincidence and déjà vu, to name a few. Like the childhood hide-and-seek game, Magical Breadcrumbs are hidden, and you're it!

The book you are holding in your hand is a Magical Breadcrumb. Follow the morsels throughout the pages of this book, and you will see the magic that has been surrounding you your entire life. Continue to follow them, and you will be led to joy and happiness as you move closer to your destiny and life's purpose.

Undoubtedly, the path of Magical Breadcrumbs is more easily seen looking back from where you are. Throughout this book, I'll continue to share my identified Magical Breadcrumbs to help you see that although something may have felt coincidental or ordinary at the time or to others, with this new perspective, it will become more apparent that these were intended Magical Breadcrumbs. We will explore why Magical Breadcrumbs are left unseen, how to increase the odds of seeing them, and how life changes when you follow Magical Breadcrumbs and let your soul lead your choices of free will. The trail stops where you stand. To continue your journey, just follow the Magical Breadcrumbs.

Give it a chance. Open yourself to recognizing Magical Breadcrumbs and watch your life change.

Reflection Section

Pause and reflect on the importance of the information I shared with you. Just by simply believing in Magical Breadcrumbs, you have the power to change your life. When you believe, you bring yourself into conscious awareness of the current time and place and become present in each moment, opening yourself to all the possibilities presented before you. And these moments, right now, are literal gifts from the Universe to you.

How do you feel about the concept of Magical Breadcrumbs? Do you believe? If so, congratulations. You are well on your way to where Source intended you to go. Continue reading. If you have yet to believe, you likely have some unidentified blockages. What do you think is standing in your way of moving forward with believing in your Magical Breadcrumbs?

_____

_____

_____

_____

_____

_____

_____

Now get comfortable and close your eyes and imagine your perfect life. The one you would live in if there wasn't anything standing in your way. What do you see? Where are you? How do you feel? What are you doing? Dare to dream and allow your imagination to run wild. This is your vision of heaven on Earth, made up of the wishes stemming from your soul. Dare to dream and allow your true heart's desire to arise because if you can imagine it, you can obtain it. Wishes and dreams are Magical Breadcrumbs too.

Chapter 5

Veils of Illusion

You have the power to choose which beliefs you hold.

Beliefs are the single most challenging factor in how we lead our lives. Beliefs in how we should act, what we should and should not do, and what is acceptable and unacceptable only begin to scratch the surface of how they affect our lives. Beliefs influence every decision you make. There is nothing simple about beliefs. They are complex, complicated, essential, and deserve our full attention, yet they are so smoothly introduced that we unknowingly latch onto them. At some point in existence, through exposure or relationships or energetically, you believed in things, and now those beliefs control how you lead your life. But you have the power to choose which beliefs you hold.

Acceptance is believing, and once beliefs are accepted, many lie invisible, operating within your subconscious, limiting you, and influencing your everyday thoughts and actions. They remain virtually undetected and possibly even dormant until a situation arises that calls the belief into action and moves you in a direction toward or against something.

Beliefs are acquired throughout your life through culture, society, family, religion, and media, but some are more deeply engrained into your soul. In fact, one of the reasons that you are accepting or rejecting my theory of Magical Breadcrumbs can be attributed to beliefs. So, let's look at where beliefs originate. Because where there is awareness, there is the amazing opportunity to recognize, analyze and consciously choose if a belief is one that you want dictating the course of your life. But first, we must understand the connection between beliefs and cognitive dissonance.

Cognitive Dissonance

Cognitive dissonance occurs when you are subjected to something that is in opposition to one or more of your held beliefs. Typically, it is one's own actions that cause cognitive dissonance. Cognitive dissonance causes emotions to arise within you, and you feel angry, disappointed, guilty, confused, conflicted, or uncomfortable. These feelings require conscious action to resolve. It is an internal disagreement one encounters with themselves when a situation or action does not align with one's beliefs, and everyone has experienced it.

This internal challenge requires one of three actions to resolve. Change or reduce the importance of the existing belief or add a new belief. Although cognitive dissonance may not feel good and be unwelcome, this is an opportunity to recognize a belief you may or may not have realized and then evaluate if it is one you want to hold or if it should be released or revised. This is a chance to redirect the power of external influences that have shaped your beliefs. A reclaiming of personal power that provides you with the freedom to choose, express your individuality, and live by your self-governance.

The following five-step belief evaluation process will guide you through the actions to take proactively or when faced with incidences of cognitive dissonance. Taking the time to address beliefs aligns one's actions with values and removes barriers to Magical Breadcrumbs. Oh, and there's no coincidence that the acronym for the process is DRAMA. Because conflicts with beliefs often cause drama internally and with those around you!

Belief Evaluation Process (DRAMA):

- **D-** Discover the belief you hold. Look beyond the surface, the apparent belief, and try to find the root of the belief. Often, beliefs lie within layers of other related beliefs.
- **R-** Recognize how the existence of the belief affects your life. Identify how each belief dictates physical, social, and emotional actions. A belief that may seem simple often reaches into areas unrecognized that limit your potential.
- **A-** Analyze each belief, including its origination and impact on your life. Stop and see if it resonates within you. Do not rush to decide. Take all the time you need to make these evaluations.
- **M-** Make a choice if the belief is one you want to hold, release, or change. These are your beliefs, but they are undoubtedly going to transform relationships.

Converse openly with those involved in your decisions to prevent conflicts.
- **A-** Acknowledge how the belief aligns with your values and purpose. Be aware of how the belief impacts your life. From here forward, act and make conscious choices, reinforcing the beliefs representing your true self.

Last, understand that beliefs can and will likely change throughout your life based on growth, personal experiences, and life circumstances. One should show grace toward yourself and allow the evolution of beliefs to continue to align with the ever evolving you, regardless of the resistance or opinions of others around you.

Personal Connection to Cognitive Dissonance

Unsurprisingly, my actions with my Twin Flame raised issues of cognitive dissonance within me. The primary belief that was challenged was that one should be faithful in marriage. I thought I believed it as well. After all, it is in the marital vows and an expectation of society. Yet, when presented with the experience, my actions were inconsistent, and evidence of cognitive dissonance arose within me.

All my decisions in the Twin Flame Journey were made from my heart, and whereas my previous belief was black and white, I discovered a gray area. A Twin Flame relationship is a soul union, and a spouse is an ego union. Both are founded and held within a space of love; one does not detract from the other. My changed belief is that both relationships can exist simultaneously.

However, when I looked deeper, I realized I had formed a new belief, one that surprised me. Having multiple partners while married is acceptable when the committed partners knowingly consent to a polyamorous lifestyle. This eliminates deception and, therefore, does not jeopardize or hurt one's relationship and spouse. This new belief stems from my realization that society has portrayed a spouse as 'the one.' The one person that is supposed to fulfill all your needs, wants, and desires forever, and my experience led me to see and feel otherwise.

Although many will disagree with my reasoning, the beauty of cognitive dissonance is that you have the power to analyze the original belief and determine how it can apply in your life unopposed. Unlike other blanket, shared beliefs held by larger populations, when one customizes and chooses a belief, it becomes a reflection of your soul's expression.

Remember, Magical Breadcrumbs will lead you toward your highest good and destiny. That does not mean they are always what your ego self and other humans want.

Soul Imprint Beliefs

Soul imprints are a transference between the soul and the ego; carried within the soul and brought into each lifetime. A belief or a feeling without identifiable origins. Soul imprints are acknowledged as phrases heard in society and are generally not disputed when people say them. They are commonly accepted as a possibility. This is because the human mind processes them somewhere between the ego and religion, so emotional triggering is usually avoided.

Source imprints are information carried over from the time of creation between Source to soul and then from soul to human. These foundational beliefs are engrained within, so those that recognize their existence just accept them as truth, while some cling to them with hope, and others are purely not aware of them. These exist within all of us, although we may not realize them. Reading this text will likely rouse people of their inner knowingness.

Emotional imprints are remnants left over by intense emotions felt during a previous human experience that remain part of the soul for eternity. Although most of us do not consciously remember what transpired prior to this incarnation or within us during early childhood years, it does not mean events did not happen that left lasting beliefs or imprints such as love, admiration, abundance, and fears, anger, guilt, lack and shame on our souls that are evident in one's actions today. And by the way, if you just doubted existence in a previous lifetime, it's because of an engrained belief, most likely revolving around religion, which we will discuss in a future section.

The important thing to remember in this chapter is that within each of us there are beliefs that we cannot pinpoint the time in which we began to believe in them because we have simply always believed.

Soul Imprint #1- Everything Happens for a Reason

Stop and think for a moment; what if there is a reason everything happens? Imagine how your life would be different if one tiny detail hadn't occurred. This concept can be challenging to consider and may trigger strong emotional reactions within those aware of endured childhood traumas, accidents, untimely deaths of loved ones, divorce, and other unpleasant experiences. But I encourage you to keep an open mind, as growth, reclaiming personal power, and unrecognized beliefs may lie here.

At the core of my being is the belief that everything happens for a reason and there are no coincidences. Good or bad, positive, or negative, there is happenstance and purpose surrounding everything. Just because our human minds cannot comprehend them does not mean our souls do not. Although the reasons are not always easily seen or immediately identified.

Explore this hypothetical scenario. Your car breaks down. Sure, you would be frustrated and possibly angry. It delayed you from your destination. But what if your car breaking down left you stuck on the side of the road to avoid a collision that would have happened if your trip continued on your timeframe? Regardless of the severity of the collision, there are always effects from accidents that change the future; no transportation, inconvenience, financial hardships, bodily injury, and even death. The mechanical failure prevented the accident from ever happening. So, don't be upset that you are late, but rather be thankful that you arrived safely. Breaking down happened for a reason and believing everything happens for a reason allows one to look at each incident and find the positives, even in what appears at first glance to be a perceived negative situation.

Believing that everything happens for a reason also provides the perspective that the good and the bad things that happen in life are all part of a bigger plan. I'm not saying I don't get upset or ask why something happened. I'm just saying that whatever the event is that happened was necessary in the big picture. Maybe it was a lesson for your soul, maybe it had to happen to put you on another path, or maybe it had nothing to do with you and you were helping someone else. It's not always about you. Say that out loud, "It's not always about me." Then look from another perspective of someone else involved and try to imagine the impact on them. Unfortunately, society teaches us to be selfish and put ourselves first, so we think of the impact on ourselves, asking why me? Or how am I so lucky? But there are always at least two sides to a story, so try to look from the other side and see that everything happens for a reason.

Personal Connection to Everything Happens for a Reason

Looking back, I recognize the first memory that I believed everything happened for a reason was at the age of four, when my family was moving from Northern California to Nevada. I remember wanting to stay in the place I had grown to love. It was home and there that I can recall my earliest, most fond memories with my mother. Surrounded by the lush vegetation of wine country, she gardened and shared her love of flowers and nature with me. Adventures were had sneaking onto the golf course to watch the ducks swim in the ponds and the bunnies hop around. We traveled to nearby beaches, enjoyed the sand and cool breezes, and explored the tidepools left behind in the sand after high tide. She showed me how to live in the moment and appreciate nature's beauty. Two of the core foundations of spirituality and following one's soul journey and opening to the possibilities of Magical Breadcrumbs.

The deep appreciation of nature has remained within me and has continued to grow. I still relish every opportunity to admire a pretty flower, watch wildlife, or put my feet into the sand. But even at such a young age, I remember telling myself we had to go, that there was a reason beyond the obvious. I choose to feel grateful for my experiences there.

Reflection Section

Pause and reflect on the soul imprint that everything happens for a reason. Does a situation come to mind that you chalk up to the possibility that it happened for a reason, although you may or may not be able to comprehend it?

Ponder the thought that everything happens for a reason. Can you see where believing this draws awareness to the positives within circumstances and the ability to see outside one's perspective and accept what is? Acknowledging that there is a bigger picture to life and that we are all interconnected, opens the possibility of receiving Magical Breadcrumbs.

_____

_____

_____

_____

_____

_____

_____

Realize there is an underlying belief to your reflection. If you reject the concept, analyze where your thoughts stem from. Then, evaluate the belief and determine if you wish to retain or revise it.

Soul Imprint #2- Meant to Be

Have you ever tried not to let something happen, and it still happened? Maybe not immediately, but eventually. Despite your best attempt to control circumstances, it just happens. What if I told you those times are directly linked to your soul's lessons and experiences? It was planned, and the free will of yourself and others could not have prevented it. Sure, they can delay or alter it, but they cannot prevent it from happening. You may know this as the commonly accepted term of fate. Everything happens for a reason, leading to what is meant to be.

Before this lifetime, our souls chose the lessons and experiences we have. I know this may be difficult to grasp if you have encountered devastation in your life, but to our souls, each opportunity sounded fun and exciting as they are unaware of the polarities that would be experienced once on the human journey.

To fulfill these choices, our souls made agreements with other souls, known as soul contracts. Soul contracts are intertwined with those of others, leaving it difficult to distinguish whether an incident was part of your plan or part of someone else's. It is an exchange of favors agreed to as souls to help someone learn a lesson or have an experience. Soul contracts can exist between you and anyone that you cross paths with within this lifetime, including but not limited to the homeless guy on the street, the barista at the local coffee shop, a lover, or a friend. The magic is in the fact that no one knows at the time. But when words or actions happen at seemingly random times strike a chord or when meeting someone elicits feelings of resonance and an undeniable deep inner knowing, these are signs of something meant to be that are Magical Breadcrumbs leading you on your path.

Explore this hypothetical scenario of an incident that shows a chain reaction involving multiple people, leading to something meant to be:

You called in sick to work, and a co-worker had to stay late to cover your shift. This caused the co-worker at the last minute to cancel plans and the babysitter she hired for her blind date. The babysitter was then forced to back out of a weekend trip because she didn't have enough money, missing the opportunity of a lifetime. However, while the blind date was left waiting at the restaurant, he met the woman of his dreams.

Seemingly insignificant, but the journeys for multiple people were realigned with the assistance of soul contracts, all because the blind date was meant to meet the woman. Although it was nearly impossible to see the ending of my make-believe story, the importance is recognizing and being able to see how this applies to your life. Our actions impact the journeys of our and other people's lives. That is not something that should be taken lightly.

Personal Connection to Meant to Be

Remember the story I started about the gut feeling that I just had to meet the guy cruising the strip? Well, here's the rest of the story. It turns out that gut feeling led me to what was meant to be.

We drifted apart. Life continued, and occasionally he crossed my mind, but nothing felt unusual. I chalked it up to a fling and moved on with my life. But, a few months into our separation, he had a run-in with a light pole after a night out with his friends. His car was severely damaged, but thankfully, he wasn't injured. I was the first person he thought to call. I went to him in the middle of the night, and it was like we never separated. But within a few months, we drifted again.

But fate came back around, and this time, I was in an automobile accident, and he was the one I wanted to console me. It was then we recognized that an unseeable force was connecting us, and we made a conscious decision to pursue our relationship. That was nearly 30 years ago.

Looking back on the entire story, I can see Magical Breadcrumbs aligning for months before we finally met.

1- Making a new friend.
2- Deciding to cruise the strip.
3- Him telling me to smile.
4- Waking in the night thinking about him.
5- The overwhelming feeling I made a mistake.
6- His car accident.
7- My car accident.

We might not have been united if any of those breadcrumbs had not occurred. And this doesn't even touch on the fact that my then-new friend also met her future husband. Everything is interconnected. We all like to think that it's our life and we are free to make our own choices, but on some level, every choice affects someone else.

Reflection Section

Pause and reflect on things in your life that would not have occurred or would be different if one thing hadn't happened. If you have children, this is easy. If you hadn't had sex at that minute with that person, your child would not have been created. You may have conceived at another time, perhaps even with the same person, but your child would not be the same individual they would have been. But look deeper. Think back to a pivotal moment when you can see how your life or circumstances would be different if one thing hadn't happened. An indicator is associated with thoughts like, "I was lucky when this happened." Or "It was just bad luck." What if your life is following a master plan, and those events or circumstances had to happen for you to learn your soul lessons and lead you to something else?

_____

_____

_____

_____

_____

_____

_____

_____

_____

You have probably heard the phrase, 'Hindsight is 20/20.' When looking back on situations, Magical Breadcrumbs are often identifiable. They are clear indicators, like 20/20 perfect vision from the Universe, providing an understanding of how or why something happened the way it did. The Universe was attempting to lead you toward your higher good and ultimate destination. Although some memories may not feel pleasant, they are all Magical Breadcrumbs.

Cultural Beliefs

Every day of our lives, we are subjected to beliefs instilled upon us by those surrounding us. Because most come from people we know and trust or because they have been handed down for generations, most believe them without question. Instead, we let them unconsciously and sometimes consciously determine choices in our lives. This results in the perpetuation of passing them to future generations.

Here are just a couple of examples to jumpstart your thinking:

1. The famous eighteenth-century nursery rhyme, What All the World is Made Of, by Robert Southey, states that little girls are made of "sugar and spice and everything nice," while little boys are made of "snips and snails and puppy dog tails." Indicating differences in gender roles and inferring how each is expected to act. This nursery rhyme has been handed down for many generations, and in some cultures,

it dictates parenting styles and how children are raised, disciplined, and expected to behave.

I feel confident saying that all of us, regardless of gender, are a combination of both. We may have more of one than the other, but no one falls into a neat category of each trait all the time, and we shouldn't have to. Beware; limiting beliefs tend to lie here, based on inferred gender roles of what one can or can't do and should or shouldn't do.

2. Little boys are tough and shouldn't show pain or emotions. Men often tell young boys phrases like, "Don't cry," "You're tough," and "It doesn't hurt that bad," implying to them they shouldn't feel things that hurt, that it is bad or wrong, all the while they see little girls crying and being comforted, creating defining lines of acceptance between the genders and enforcing the differences between them.

Because all children want their parents' love and approval, they do their best to start hiding their signs of pain. Stifling emotions and burying feelings becomes routine, and they carry those lessons into adulthood; and suddenly, we have a world full of men who are removed from the very things this journey is about, the feelings associated with the lessons and experiences. And to make matters worse, they perpetuate the cycle with their children. Beware; more false beliefs lie here in gender inequality and gender roles, as well as in the widening gap between the ego and the soul.

3. Another example is the belief that going outside with wet hair will make you catch a cold. Going outside with wet hair might make you uncomfortable in the cold weather, but it can't give you a cold.

However, the wet hair may have contributed to worsening symptoms of a virus you had, but just having damp hair and going outside will make no one catch a cold. A superstition or myth handed down for generations based on false information.

Hopefully, these got you thinking, but to fully grasp this category, you must look at all the layers of culture each of us is part of that influence us and understand that the color of our skin, our sexuality, or any other identifying characteristic does not determine our fate. Just because we identify with a culture does not mean we are the same. There are no two people completely identical. However, at the root of all cultural levels, are a group of people that can relate to one another. It is essential to recognize that lying underneath each one of the shared characteristics of cultures are beliefs, and those beliefs can limit your Magical Breadcrumbs.

To simplify, think about this; acceptable behavior with your friends is likely to differ from behavior with your parents, and how you dress at work is likely different than what you wear on your time off. Use the feelings of having to act in a certain way as an indicator to delve deeper into the belief behind it.

Yes, we all have things in common, and you may look the same on the outside or trace your DNA roots to the same lineage. But many other factors contribute to your unique culture, including origination, where you live, languages you speak, family order, religion, occupation, recreational and lifestyle choices, and people you surround yourself with.

Each one of these layers comes with beliefs attached. But remember, to hold a belief, you had to believe it at some point. If you have heard a belief since childhood or felt the impact of acceptance or rejection of those surrounding you, you likely perpetuate the cycle by role-modeling it or even saying it aloud. I intend to draw your awareness to the areas that deserve a closer look to unveil unrecognized beliefs. You may choose to hold or release them, but your understanding will allow the reclaiming of personal power that may have been inadvertently relinquished.

Personal Connection to Cultural Beliefs

As a young, impressionable girl growing up in Las Vegas, I was surrounded by images of scantily clad women. In a place with a reputation for being 'Sin City,' marketing images on top of taxi cabs, billboards, and television portrayed women as sex symbols wearing revealing clothing, bronzed skin, toned bodies, and large breasts. These images unknowingly built a belief within me of a woman who was grown, sexy, and desirable. Consequently, my body, which did not reflect those images, felt inadequate, leading me to consider plastic surgery and thinking I had never grown up. For me, it wasn't about how old I was or my marital status; it was about an image of appearance that determined maturity and desirability based upon false beliefs.

Reflection Section

Pause and reflect on just one culture you belong to. Can you identify one of the group's beliefs you are subjected to? How does that belief impact you inside and outside of the group? What do you discover when you analyze it using the Belief Evaluation Process? Do you believe it? Why or why not?

_____

_____

_____

_____

_____

_____

_____

_____

Often, societal and cultural beliefs are followed to fit in, and failing to do so creates false limiting beliefs about our abilities and the fear of failure, creating layers of separation from your Magical Breadcrumbs! We allow our ego minds to protect us from judgment, and fear dictates how we lead our lives. And before you know it, all your actions are based on some level of belief. I beg you to recognize each one, analyze its origination, and choose if it is what you want to follow. This alone will change your life. But it also clears the path for Magical Breadcrumbs to appear.

Programming Beliefs

All our lives, we are subjected to institutions that form and instill our beliefs, woven into the fabric of our existence that lay behind societal structures and necessities. Most have been there as long as we can remember and appear to provide advantages. They are buried within educational, financial, healthcare, and social systems, the government, and the media.

Each of these layers deserves closer attention and analysis. Behind all organized systems is the goal of providing for the masses. On the surface, they provide knowledge, money, healthcare, or information. But underneath, they are programming everyone to think the same and rely upon sources outside of ourselves, raising opportunities to create false beliefs about our individuality, abilities, and purpose. Each program takes you further from your intuitiveness about what aligns with your heart's truth and distracts you from Source connection and your Magical Breadcrumbs.

Although your beliefs already persuade your thoughts in this chapter, I turn your attention to the people behind the systems. Some earn honest livings, selflessly serve others for the greater good, and then some have found abilities within systems to propel their personal agendas. These are people rooted in ego who are disconnected from Source, purpose, and their heart and soul. They utilize false trust and coercion to manipulate and control the population with filtered and selected information. My point is not to turn you against so-called leaders but to stop blindly believing what you hear or following along with what others say because the beliefs you hold of them tell you to. Recognize the programs, critically analyze them, and decide what you believe.

Any time you are forced to participate in something, investigate the motive. When you hear something, examine why it is being said. When people are shown acting against one another, or standing out as an identified label, investigate the issue. Through blind faith and accepting things as just the way they are, you are instilling the beliefs forced upon you instead of actively choosing.

The key to seeing into these beliefs is looking closely whenever you feel fear. What is the motive behind someone wanting to make you and others feel fearful? The emotion of fear is one of the lowest and most controlling vibrations humans can experience. Unfortunately, many leaders and systems use fear to disguise lies, corruption, and personal agendas.

Power lies here. A quote by Edmund Burke, an eighteenth-century philosopher, warns, "The greater the power, the more dangerous the abuse." It is the power that commonly leads media and programming beliefs. Mr. Burke's statement should be seen as an indicator and warning to all of us to consider further hidden agendas in what we see and hear because the beliefs of being imprisoned and controlled lie here.

Have you noticed more and more people are being divided and labeled? Races, sexualities, economic status, and political affiliations are becoming more widely accepted to be put into smaller groups, segregating people. Division lies here.

Winston Churchill, one of the most famous politicians ever, said, "United we stand, divided we fall." By accepting a subgroup into society, we potentially isolate ourselves, creating a more significant imbalance of power and a perception of lack and inequality. Although individually, we may feel liberated; we must not overlook the importance of accepting and tolerating others, especially if they appear different. Together we rise.

Where the distribution of power is unbalanced, beliefs and circumstances can isolate people and give more power to institutions through perceived needs. False impressions of discrimination, hate, isolation, and powerlessness breed here. When we come together as one, our strength magnifies opportunities to recognize and embrace what we each bring to one another and the human experience.

Personal Connection to Programming Beliefs

Although the topic is controversial, the Coronavirus pandemic changed the lives of everyone in the world overnight. People were isolated from the very things that are essential to thrive in this journey. It is not a matter of whether you believe in the virus, mask-wearing, quarantining, or in the vaccine. It is about how you reacted to the situation, based upon the selected and filtered information you received from those holding the power of programming your beliefs during and long before. Those beliefs determined the choices you made.

I do not doubt the existence of the virus as I survived it. Those I love have had it, and I know people that perished. But this is about consciously choosing what you believe is right for you and not being mindlessly led by forces of false beliefs and low vibrational energy, including intimidation, fear, and power. To isolate, to wear a mask, to take a vaccine, each of those decisions are for you to make based on beliefs you choose to hold. But regardless of your choice, the priority should be tolerance, acceptance and respect of others who may not choose to react as you do because they hold alternative beliefs.

Reflection Section

Pause and reflect on at least one area you identify as making you feel fear or divided. If you find yourself feeling fearful, forced to do things, or lumped into a group or labeled, it is time to look at the underlying causes and impacts on your belief system. Is your thought based on truth, or is it one that someone else may have used to manipulate you? Are you choosing to accept and continue to follow it or release it and let it go, as it does not align with your truth?

_____

_____

_____

_____

_____

_____

_____

Limiting your exposure to mass programming is essential. Turning off the television, stepping away from the computer, and putting down your smartphone prevents unnecessary subjectivity to negativity and stops the programming flow. Instead, engage with others, make organic connections, and experience life. These are essential for seeing your truth and recognizing Magical Breadcrumbs!

Business Beliefs

Everywhere we turn, someone is trying to sell us something. Worldwide, businesses employ millions of people in marketing products and services, intending to convince each of us we need or want something they offer to increase their profitability.

Greed. Referred to in the common phrase, "The root of all evil," is lying here. In the process of creating sales and increasing the bottom line through marketing campaigns, people, especially children and women, are brainwashed into believing that buying this will fix you, solve your problem, or make you happier. Campaigns are designed to sound like they are helping you, but they are master manipulators that want your hard-earned money, and your existing beliefs may make you an easy target.

The world has become centered around consumerism and making money, often at the expense of the health and well-being of the inhabitants and our Earth. We cannot escape the presence of businesses, but we can recognize vulnerabilities within us that make us susceptible to believing what they are saying and make lifestyle choices that limit our exposure. Marketing campaigns are filling our heads with things that are not true unless we believe them. Remember, it takes believing to make it a belief. The false beliefs of 'I am not enough' are commonly hidden here. But now that your perception of the motive behind sales, marketing, and business has been widened, you can recognize and choose not to make purchases based on an unfounded reason.

Conscious awareness of the underlying messages and realizing that advertising is priming and programming you to believe claims with ulterior motives allows you to think critically about each advertisement, revealing the truth and preventing you from buying into false beliefs and wasting money. But if you find yourself tempted and falling for their sales tactics, force yourself to wait 30 days before purchasing.

During the 30 days:

- ✓ Research motives- Give yourself time to identify why you want this product or service and whether it is based on a genuine need, a falsely created need, or a belief that you lack something within you. Look closely at the feelings that arise within you when you see it advertised and determine if your want lies in how it will make you feel. Often, feelings uncover beliefs. Avoid making a purchase based on an emotional decision founded on untruth.
- ✓ Research the product- Determine if the product or service can meet its advertising claims, or is another product better suited for you? Avoid needlessly spending money repeatedly for similar items, as it indicates desperation to repair a feeling or belief or feeble attempts to control a result and not address the cause.
- ✓ Research the manufacturer and retailers- Are you proud to financially support the maker and the sellers, or are there other more deserving options? Consider the environmental impact of each and recognize that purchases with a big box business add to their profitability. While shopping with local and smaller businesses directly supports those in your community, which likely reflects your similar values and culture.

Try following these steps, and you'll be surprised that most purchases will never happen. You have absolutely nothing to lose! Besides, this is also a great way to role model and teach children the concepts of delayed gratification and critical thinking and instill lifelong spending habits. While at the same time, opportunities arise for you to address false beliefs and uncover Magical Breadcrumbs.

Personal Connection to Business Beliefs

You may remember the thigh gap controversy of the 2010s. Businesses were called out for photoshopping images of models to make them fit their definition of appealing and attractive. Unfortunately, the effects run much deeper, especially for those who are impressionable or insecure about themselves—the models and photos used in marketing campaigns subliminally program viewers' body images. How one sees, feels, and thinks about their body and subsequent actions are likely reflections of subjection to years of programming by those trying to sell you products or services.

Don't always believe what you see. The power of modern technology allows for digital enhancement, including slimming thighs and midsections, smoothing skin tones, removing aging lines, enhancing bust sizes, and the list goes on as common practices. Although I have resisted believing I must look like that, I am programmed to observe how specific areas of my body look, especially my thighs.

Pause and reflect on the products you have purchased in the past, prompted by marketing and advertising promising to improve your life, make you more attractive, or fix a problem.

Can you see where you were led to think that you needed something because you believed them only to line the pockets of the business? Identify one product you fell for. Why did you buy it? What emotions did it make you feel? What was the underlying belief? If you had known the 3-step, 30-day pause process, would you have bought it?

_____

_____

_____

_____

_____

_____

_____

_____

It comes back to limiting your exposure. Stopping mindless scrolling on social media and watching television helps prevent the creation of new false beliefs and the solidification of current ones and saves you money. You are created divinely perfect, and no product makes you more perfect than you already are.

Religious Beliefs

With over 80% of the world's population identifying as following a religion, and countless different faiths, it is very easy to see where many beliefs lie. And you don't have to look very far to see where sometimes people's religious beliefs cause violence and discrimination against others simply because they believe differently.

Religion is a topic that encompasses every aspect of the human journey. In simple terms, religion is what people consider holy and sacred, but to truly comprehend the complexity, one must consider that many religions regard written books as having scriptural status, the beliefs that dictate how people live their lives, one's fate after death and those that designate people as leaders of divine guidance. Religion also defines how one's relationship and attitude toward God/Spirit is regarded and, in some religions, also includes interactions between people and nature. Then, you must consider how people worship; prayer, rituals, and meditation are common. Some of these are isolated practices, while others are done in groups. Each religion holds beliefs and has established moral standards and expectations of appropriate and desired behavior. There are infinite possibilities to disagree with others' views and to experience cognitive dissonance when one's life choices do not align with their religious beliefs.

Religions are interpretations. As seen in the childhood game of telephone, where everyone stands in a line, and the first person whispers something into the ear of the person next to them, and then that person shares what they heard with the next person until it reaches the end of the line. The ending message is always different from the beginning; It has been interpreted how they heard it. In addition, when humans apply their own ears, minds, and ego interpretations to what they hear, other beliefs are set. This is a possibility of how religious texts and congregations evolve over time and layers of beliefs are established. The closer an individual is to Source, the more purity lies in the messages.

Confinements

Some of the most remarkable connections to Source are missed within the confinements of the beliefs under one's claimed religious affiliation. Too often, people follow the religion of their past family lineage instead of genuinely choosing for themselves. Claiming a religion or failing to actively do so sets one up for great cognitive dissonance with the connected beliefs throughout their life. When one's choices do not align with the beliefs of their religion, guilt arises as "I should be doing..." or "I shouldn't be doing..." Fear looms of what happens for not obeying "Will I still go to heaven?" and shame "I've let others down" not doing as I was told or shown. Each of these low vibrations are the furthest from Source's love and light can be avoided by consciously choosing your faith and shedding false and limiting beliefs.

Religion can prevent people from believing and receiving Magical Breadcrumbs. Although it may sound like a contradiction, as religion is supposed to bring one closer to Source, sometimes the hidden beliefs in religion get unintentional and undesired outcomes where you least expect it. Some examples include those who have endured traumas in their lives they believe God would not allow to happen, like abuse, neglect, abandonment, untimely death of loved ones, and other unfortunate circumstances, and then different beliefs are often buried deep within and appear seemingly harmless like not lighting candles, dancing, or having archangel statues in one's home. Each and every belief you hold surrounding religion holds the possibility of confining your potential connection to Source and the ability to receive Magical Breadcrumbs.

Just as people speak many different languages, people interpret the Universe in the language that was culturally presented to them, which may not necessarily resonate with their souls. One's relationship with the higher power you believe in is intimate. Listen to your heart and its resonance, and be guided by the love and connection within you. The rest, including the limiting and false beliefs, will be released, allowing your faith to fall into place.

Personal Connection to Religious Beliefs

Although I was introduced to religion through my grandfather in his Southern Baptist Church, the messages and method of worship seemed confining and obligatory and did not resonate with my heart. However, the sense of community and the caring and praying I saw the people do together felt natural and heartwarming. It resonated within me, but the method and place of worship did not.

This does not mean I wasn't interested in the messages being delivered in church; I just needed to hear them in a language, place, and way I could relate to and absorb them. My mother found the secret to delivering the words of Source to my ears and heart. While in elementary school, my mom would pick me up at lunchtime, and we would sit under the shade of a tree, eating lunch and reciting the Biblical stories she learned growing up in the church. I found resonance in the messages of the Bible through those times we spent together, and I realized I didn't have to attend services to connect with the Universe; I had a direct link to the connection, and I could worship anywhere and anytime I wanted to. From a very young age, I could see the roadblocks of religion and chose to follow my heart.

Reflection Section

Pause and reflect on your thoughts and beliefs surrounding religion. An excellent place to start is when you feel guilt, shame, or fear for things you do or don't do. Even if you are one of the minority of people who do not identify as following a religion, I guarantee you hold beliefs surrounding religion. Write down your views. How do they impact your life today?

_____

_____

_____

_____

_____

_____

_____

_____

Now, ask yourself, do you want to hold those beliefs? Letting go of individual beliefs or an entire religion and establishing new ones is perfectly acceptable. This often happens when a situation has shown you otherwise or an established belief no longer aligns with you. Let go of any guilt or fear revolving around changing your perspective. The Greek Philosopher Heraclitus said it best when he said, "Change is the only constant in life." Change is natural, and just because the outcome is unknown does not mean it will be for the worse. Please think of the seasons and when they change. Each season holds its own beauty and purpose that should not be compared to what came before or will come after.

Chapter 6

Breakthrough the Barriers

By now, you should realize that everyone has Magical Breadcrumbs. They are always around us; it is just a matter of whether you are tapped into receiving. We have explored the common areas where beliefs may lie as barriers, but now we must reveal how to breakthrough those barriers and empower ourselves to claim our divine guidance.

Anything is possible when you just believe.

Recognizing Equal Opportunities

We live in a time with laws protecting sex, age, color, race, religion, disability, national origin, and gender identity, yet discrimination still exists. And where discrimination exists, there are lower vibrational energies like hate, anxiety, guilt, anger, fear, jealousy, inferiority, and violence. But it does not have to be this way. As souls, we have equal opportunities.

Imagine for a moment how different life would be if we each shed the layers of what identifies us. The indifferences judged superficially by others would be dissolved instantly, eliminating discrimination. Our souls would be exposed, leaving only divine perfection. Think about the peace this would bring.

Now, I know you might be thinking, "This is my life; I just have to deal with it," or "I am right where I wanted to be at this point in my life," or "I am too old to change." Anything is possible when you believe. It is never too late to reach for what you want. You have free will, and you can choose to continue with your current existence and follow the trajectory of your life or break the cycle and reach for the stars. Either way, at least analyze who you think you are and who I know you to be. An entire Universe exists within you in beauty, truth, and freedom that you can harness and change your life and leave your mark in the world!

Take a moment to think about the layers of your identity that you perceive as making you who you are. Here is a list of some to help jumpstart your brainstorming, but please do not let these limit you.

- Skin color
- Gender

- Sexual orientation
- Ethnicity
- Religion
- Marital status
- Profession
- Socioeconomic status
- Culture
- Family

Now, look at your list of identity layers and think about shedding each one. No longer allowing yourself to be identified as black or white, gay or straight, someone's husband or wife, mom or dad, sister or brother, a lawyer or cashier, Catholic or Mormon, and so on. It is likely that just thinking about this concept is raising some resistance within you or triggering you to discredit my views. Push past those feelings; each are indications that your ego is fighting to control your existence.

I know it feels scary to even think about this concept. But realizing why you think, feel, and act as you do is necessary to recognize your Magical Breadcrumbs.

Personal Connection to Equal Opportunity

A few years ago, my husband and I packed up our children and headed for a new life in coastal Oregon. But, before I left, I experienced an ego death. I was numbly going through the final times of routine activities in my life that defined my identity; last days at work, final Cub Scout meetings, saying goodbye to friends and family, last cups of coffee, and car washes at my favorite places. Although there was great sadness and grief around many endings, I was releasing all the labels I had held onto, and a new opportunity to reinvent myself emerged. I could be anyone or anything I chose without obligation or concern for what others wanted or thought. Within me, there was excitement about the new beginning, the adventures awaiting, and a future of possibilities and the unknown.

Most labels that identified me had been stripped, and their shadows were dissolved. It was then that I explored myself, and I started discovering who I was beneath my ego and what everyone else could see on the outside, and to my surprise, Magical Breadcrumbs started to appear.

Reflection Section

Pause and reflect for a moment. What are your identities? What do you think would happen to you if you shed them? Just a warning that natural tendencies will cause you to list negatives first because you can measure what you can lose; dig deeper and find the positives. For this to be highly effective, consider tangible changes, feelings, and emotions.

_____

_____

_____

_____

_____

_____

Looking within and shedding your ego, false beliefs, and superficial identities is problematic and requires grit and determination. And it is not always roses and sunshine, but I assure you the journey and what will be gained will be beyond your wildest dreams.

Eliminating Limiting Beliefs

We all have them. Our limiting beliefs lie dormant inside us, interfering with our everyday actions. Limiting beliefs are ideas we have adopted based upon what we have been subjected to that give us false and invisible boundaries to our potential and capabilities. Although our egos create them to keep us safe, they are the barrier preventing us from reaching our true potential and destinies. Limiting beliefs are the answers to the questions of why you have not done or obtained something you say you want.

I am not enough. I do not deserve it. I am afraid of failure. I am not pretty enough. I am not ready. I am not smart enough. I am scared of the responsibilities that come with success. That's because I am a woman. I am not worthy. I don't have the experience, and the list goes on and on. These negative thoughts and lies exist within you, creating invisible barriers encasing you from reaching your potential. But most of the time, we do not see our limiting beliefs or recognize their impacts on our lives. Each is hidden somewhere deep inside the subconscious mind, operating in the background of our lives.

But what if I told you everything you think negatively about yourself isn't true? All the negative impressions, thoughts, and ideas you have of yourself stem from an opinion, a statement, or one of the beliefs you read about earlier. Maybe a comment said intentionally to hurt or just mis-communicated has stuck. Words are powerful! And at the core of our beings, the way we think, we believe them. But limiting beliefs do not just stem from words. Maybe something you saw or felt left a lasting impression. Every negative statement and situation is recorded deep inside and manifests into areas of your life where you fail to fully engage in unless you recognize and work through the emotions that arise. These prevent you from seeing and following Magical Breadcrumbs. Imagine for a moment if all those false ideas just disappeared.

Maybe it's that dream job with a high-paying salary, falling in love, or wearing a sexy little black dress or something else. Each of our limiting beliefs is established and arises differently. But once they are recognized and dispelled, our path of Magical Breadcrumbs is more easily revealed. You are absolutely none of those limiting beliefs. Your soul is free, perfect, and limitless!

Recognizing self-limiting beliefs is not an easy feat, and I must warn you that healing from them requires strength, perseverance, and commitment. But the result is worth it. You are worth it! Remove all the lies you tell yourself, and your soul's perfection is revealed to the world! And that's where the true magic happens.

The limiting beliefs stemming from abusive situations are often easily identified; however, most limiting beliefs are innocently and easily established, as I share in the personal connection.

Personal Connection to Eliminating Limiting Beliefs

At two or three years old, I was often in a position where I could not go where my much older siblings went and partake in what they did. Although, as an adult, I know I was too young or small to go, this was interpreted and retained within the child me as rejection, and I wasn't good enough. That was not the case, but an innocent account during my childhood resulted in a limiting belief that changed my social life until it was revealed and healed after forty-plus years!

I built walls to protect myself from being rejected. I didn't make new friends, and I pretended not to be interested in things most kids do. I couldn't be rejected or denied if I wasn't anyone's friend. I had a self-limiting belief that disguised Magical Breadcrumbs for decades.

Reflection Section

Pause and reflect on one thing you have wanted for a long time but have not gotten or done. It could be going back to school, meeting the love of your life, buying a new car, or getting a promotion at work. Now try to identify some of your self-limiting beliefs that may be preventing you from obtaining what you say you want. Complete a sentence beginning with "I'm not..." What is your limiting belief surrounding this want? Do you recognize where it stemmed from? Dig deep until you realize it is simply a result of something that happened that you unknowingly latched onto. Now imagine what would be different if you did not hold this self-limiting belief.

_____

_____

_____

_____

_____

_____

_____

_____

We are often our own worst enemies. Although the creation of limiting beliefs is to protect us, those very things also hurt us by preventing us from reaching our potential and manifesting the life we want. Remember, as a soul, you are divinely perfect and capable of anything. So consciously remind yourself that the identified self-belief is merely an incorrect thought you no longer believe, and that nothing is too good for you. Releasing these barriers opens doors to saying yes to Magical Breadcrumbs.

Reclaiming Personal Power

Personal power is a frame of mind, an attitude, and an ability to choose how to act and feel. It's a self-confidence that one can make choices, advocating for what one believes in, standing up for what one wants or thinks, and what one believes is in their best interest without compromising for other's needs, wants, or desires that are not shared. It is not about control or force over another, but consciously choosing to use inner strength and autonomy to lead one through life.

Each soul is equal and free to experience, but they must retain personal power to reach their destiny. Although relinquishing personal power can happen anytime during one's life, experiences from the beginning disguise one's rights and ability to exude personal power. During early childhood years, how the adults in your life treated you when you were young and dependent molded your perception of your capabilities. Children given choices, encouraged to think, and supported with guidance developed a foundation and retained their power of freedom led by love, respect, and confidence. While children who had decisions made for them and were told how to think, feel, and act became insecure, felt incapable, and were led by fears of making wrong decisions.

But as children grow into teenagers, they naturally exude their personal power. Like a compass pointing them toward their true north, their power is essential to finding joy and happiness. Those supported as young children are responsible and make good choices, while those not supported act recklessly and irresponsibly. Although it may appear to be defiance and opposition, they are learning how to apply their personal power, spread their wings, and figure out what honors the sovereignty of their soul.

We are all sovereign beings. The influences of this life create false and limiting beliefs, and subsequently, the relinquishing of personal power contributes to the concealment of our individual sovereignty. When one's personal power is not honored, feelings of being controlled and imprisoned arise, making Magical Breadcrumbs challenging to see and nearly impossible to follow.

Many times throughout our lives, we have inadvertently given away our personal power. It might look like giving in to another's wishes, trying to please others, putting someone else's desires before your own, not standing up for what you want or need, or allowing yourself to be controlled or manipulated by someone. But it doesn't usually stop at a single incident. Instead, the first often paves the way for subsequent choices that become a pattern throughout life. Recognizing you have relinquished your power is usually easy, but changing the situation or pattern and reclaiming your power can be challenging.

Through recognizing the times within your life when you relinquished personal power, you often uncover identity labels and the limiting beliefs surrounding them, widening your perspective and opening possibilities. To end the unhealthy patterns, one must make conscious choices and changes to existing relationships, starting with establishing healthy boundaries and communication. Although others may see these as detrimental to themselves, the changes are honoring your sovereignty, aligning you with your highest version of yourself and your destiny, and unlocking Magical Breadcrumbs.

For some, retaining personal power is easy, while others require constant conscious remembrance to question oneself and analyze decisions and actions to ensure they align with one's awareness and do not fall back into the old habits that have likely run the subconscious activities for many years.

Personal Connection to Reclaiming Personal Power

Reclaiming my power began when I recognized that I did not always have to agree, accommodate, or please others to keep them in my life. When I remembered my divine perfection, I realized how important this is to my joy and happiness. However, I will admit that retaining my power is an ongoing process that requires me to remain conscious of my actions and choices. But by establishing and maintaining healthy boundaries and engaging in open communication about my needs, wants, and desires, I honor my soul's sovereignty.

Reflection Section

Pause and reflect on your relationships. Can you recognize one where you need to reclaim your personal power? Why do you think you gave it away initially? Is there an underlying belief, perhaps hidden behind a label, that inadvertently led you to do it? What steps should you take to reclaim your power and sovereignty?

_____

_____

_____

_____

_____

_____

_____

_____

_____

Reclaiming your personal power is not selfish, although some underlying beliefs may try to convince you otherwise. When you listen to your higher self and make decisions, take action and set boundaries with others that honor your needs and desires, you are loving and respecting yourself. In the beginning, implementing power practices may feel uncomfortable, however, the process gets easier with time and consistency.

Finding Your Faith

Your connection to Source is a very personal, individual line of communication to be nurtured and held in the highest of importance. Treat it like establishing a new relationship with a partner or friend where you can express yourselves and support each other, unlike any other friendship.

You are the creator of your faith; you get to decide and develop the practices that make you feel connected. But beware, your hidden beliefs surrounding religion will be revealed here. Do not let them stop you from doing what your heart and your resonance feel in alignment with.

What is Your Faith?

Although the question, what is your faith is only four little words, the answer to this question is not as obvious or straightforward as it may seem. You must look within your heart and use your mind to research and analyze to develop your beliefs about life, death, and everything in between. Looking back on your reflections from the religion section in Chapter Five will also help you answer this question.

Do you find that your faith lies solely in an established religion? That the beliefs and practices held by the religion all resonate within you and your heart is open to believing everything it says through its proclaimed leaders and religious text? Can you commit yourself to all the expected practices of religion? It is imperative that the part about committing to the expectations of the religion can be followed and that you're committed 100%. Anything less than complete commitment will leave you falling prey to low vibrations, such as guilt for committing perceived sins, which block Magical Breadcrumbs. If your faith lies solely on established religion, you will be able to complete this sentence with decisiveness, conviction, and authority; I am proud to be _____. (Christian, Catholic, Jewish, Jehovah's Witness, etc...) If not, look to find your faith elsewhere.

Do you find that your faith lies outside of an established religion? That your connection is more organic and unconfined by rules and expectations? Do you believe there is something higher than oneself? Do you think that lives hold higher purposes? Do you honor relationships with other people? Hold yourself to values? Have an unexplainable connection to the Earth and celestial bodies?

If so, perhaps your faith lies in spirituality. Spirituality is a more individual, unique type of faith than religion, and the questions above do not require agreement, only acknowledgment and acceptance. Spirituality is fluidity and understanding that everything is interconnected. But beware, underlying beliefs may try to lead you into believing spirituality is the opposite of religion. If your faith lies in spirituality, you can simply say, "I know."

Do you find that your line is blurred in some hybrid between religion and spirituality? Maybe you find truth in the basis of religions but do not believe in all the teachings, requirements, or confinements. Yet, you wonder about existence and ponder the idea of a higher power. If a hybrid is right for you, you pick and choose the elements of religion and those of spirituality that resonate within you. You are not bound by rules or boundaries but follow what feels right for you. If your faith lies here, you can say, "I believe."

Do you find you don't believe in any religion or spirituality? If this describes you, I encourage you to go back to the sections on beliefs surrounding culture and religion and dig into the reasoning. At the core, you will likely uncover a belief that needs to be analyzed to determine if it is one you wish to hold. If, after you do this, you still find that you are unable to find your faith, begin exploring the science and history surrounding religion and spirituality. You are likely an individual heavily weighted by the ego that needs concrete proof of existence to believe. If your faith lies here, you can say, "I see."

Personal Connection to Finding Your Faith

I found my faith somewhere between religion and spirituality. As a child, I was introduced to religion, which sparked an interest, a curiosity, and a connection to Source. But as I grew up, I realized I believed in higher powers, but they could not be confined to one religion. I was left with more questions than answers until I began spiritually awakening.

My awakening brought clarity and understanding to what I found puzzling before. Without declaring or following a religion, I began receiving voices of guidance, including some scripture. This method of one-on-one communication solidified my belief in the Bible and the Universe and my ability to worship without religion leading me to my own personalized faith.

My faith is simple; I believe. Not because I have been told or shown what to believe by others, but because my heart and intuition have led me to my truth. I believe every living thing has value and purpose. I believe we are all interconnected, and I believe our environment is of utmost importance, and that we can each connect, manifest, and live the life of our dreams.

My scripture to live by:

"Thou shalt love the Lord thy God with all thy heart, and with all thy soul, and with all thy mind."
(Matthew 22:37 KJV)

This scripture infers each of our Lords or Gods may differ, but what matters is that you allow all of you to believe. The reference to mind ties the soul's journey and this lifetime together, indicating that alignment between the two existences is essential for surrendering to faith. My heart and soul already knew the connection; my ego, however, had become jaded and blocked by outside influences. But when they aligned, my Magical Breadcrumbs started arising.

Finding my faith comforted me. I am never alone; I am surrounded and guided by Source, angels, loved ones who have crossed, and other high vibrations. Together, we share every moment as they show, teach, tell, and lead me through life and the lessons and emotions I am here to experience. By living in the present, showing gratitude, and accepting others, I am honoring the connection and opening myself to receiving.

Finding my faith unlocked my purpose. I know my soul chose to come here at this time and in this body for an essential role in the ascension of humanity and that life continues after death, so not to take it so seriously. I permit myself to fail and to make mistakes. I show myself grace when I stumble, and I live for the moments that take my breath away and make me happy to be alive. I understand that wonderful things happen if I let faith lead the way.

My faith is my uniqueness. I can pray and meditate with others or by myself. And I can burn candles, read the Bible, use crystals, set intentions, manifest, light sage and communicate with those guiding me from the spirit realm. But most importantly, I accept these practices may change over time, leading to a greater connection and awareness. A journey of faith is not to control, but to allow the evolution of self.

Reflection Section

Pause and reflect on your faith. Do you have one established yet, or has this book gotten you thinking about and considering all the possibilities you have to develop an intimate relationship with Source? After reflecting, what is your faith? Was it already existing? Did you revise it, or is it new? Were any limiting beliefs recognized and released from the change?

_____

_____

_____

_____

_____

_____

_____

_____

_____

Finding one's faith is liberating and powerful. It brings feelings of peace to the heart. But one must remember that acceptance and tolerance of those who believe differently are essential to aligning with Magical Breadcrumbs. Just because someone believes differently does not mean it is wrong; hidden beliefs lead you to those assumptions.

Sometimes one's mind needs to be opened and their perspective widened to understand another's faith perspective. No one faith is superior, correct, or wrong; they are just different and should be honored.

Stop

Stop and think about your beliefs and what you need to strip away to rebuild your thoughts and align with your Magical Breadcrumbs. It is essential to recognize that beliefs create veils of illusions inhibiting the ability to see others, situations, and circumstances clearly. Everyone has equal opportunities to receive Magical Breadcrumbs, but sometimes it takes peeling back what you have inadvertently latched onto in this lifetime to realize you are worthy of accepting these gifts. When you release the false beliefs, reclaim your personal power, remember your sovereignty, and claim your faith, you honor your spark and open opportunities to Magical Breadcrumbs! The magic of the Universe surrounds us all the time; we just have to look at the right things to see them.

Chapter 7

Floodgates of Energy

Understanding Energy

Have you ever really stopped and thought about energy? We are all guilty of saying "I don't have the energy" referring to either the mental or emotional capacities to process a situation or the physical ability to conduct an activity. But this only begins to scratch the surface of what energy is. Without energy, the world, time, and space as we know it would not exist. Energy is the foundation of everything; it is invaluable.

Humans are falsely led to believe that money is more valuable. People spend most of their lives working to collect money; forced to spend most waking hours away from loved ones and the things that bring them joy and happiness. Money and making it provide illusions while stealing away our precious lives, but enable us to survive and strive toward the lives we envision. It's easy to see how one could be deceived into thinking it is the most important thing.

But it is energy that holds the title of the utmost highest form of currency, and one of the most valuable assets and commodities. It is not tangible, which can create a struggle for comprehension. Energy is real, free, and limitless. It can shift, change, absorb, reflect, repel, and attract without sacrificing, and it is sovereign and powerful. It is within and around us all the time. Like water, we cannot survive without it and like love, it never goes away; it just changes form.

Reflection Section

Pause and reflect on how you feel about energy. Are you surprised that energy is the most valuable and powerful asset one can have? Have you honestly ever thought about the impact of energy in your life? Does learning this information change your attitude or actions toward it?

_____

_____

_____

_____

_____

_____

_____

_____

_____

Even though money is a necessity for survival, one's attitude and energy toward money and how it impacts their relationships with others determines whether the flow is toward or against. One's relationship with money must be balanced between ego and soul fulfillment as it carries energetic vibrations and can raise or lower your energy. Think about gratefulness providing abundance and recognize that while greed may appear to provide more, the lower vibrations cause an exchange separating you from Magical Breadcrumbs.

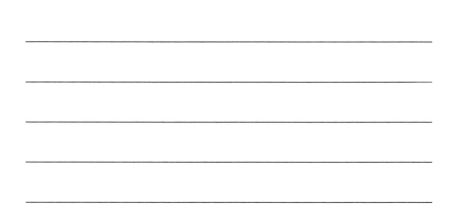

Protecting Your Energy

Energy is so valuable that it must be protected. Protecting it is essential to one's overall happiness. Treat it as a top priority, as it is the force that provides your will and sovereignty. But you still may need clarification about how energy impacts your daily life. The most obvious way we can all relate to energy is by thinking about our emotions. Although emotions can vastly differ in intensity, all emotions are energy.

Emotions are arising internal energies that cause moods to shift and reflect outward. Typically, emotions change subtly, allowing for transition and adjustment, leaving the transformation effortless and undetected, but other times, situations arise that move energies instantly. Emotions and moods are regular movements in which the flow of energy follows through the body that usually comes and goes.

Think about the last time you walked into a room and the person there was angry about something. You likely felt the change in energy when you walked in. Words and actions indicated the person's mood, but it was probably the energy radiating in the space that first alerted you to the anger. You may have even begun to feel similarly. When we allow ourselves to experience our emotions, the energy flow continues through and exits the body. However, experiencing trauma and failing to feel the associated emotions results in the energy becoming too heavy to move, and it becomes lodged within the body, resulting in unexplained ailments now or later in life. Going with the flow is essential to protecting your energy.

Protecting your energy is not selfish; it is a matter of healthy living, survival, peace, and harmony. Implementing preventative techniques like using essential oils is critical to protect your energy. Avoiding interactions with negative people, forgiving others, letting go of the past, not holding grudges, and severing ties in toxic relationships are essential. But no matter the barriers you create and the precautions you take, you are still susceptible to those surrounding you.

Sexually Transmitted Energies (STEs)

Sexually transmitted energies (STEs) are transferred the same way as STDs (sexually transmitted diseases) and STIs (sexually transmitted infections), but these lie invisibly and undetected and are virtually impossible to trace initial contraction. This might come as quite a surprise, but having sex is the highest form of transferring energy between people. When you take your clothes off with someone, you not only reveal your physical body, but the most vulnerable aspects of yourself.

Sex is a life-changing exchange of energy between partners. Not only does it have the ability to create life, but it has the natural powers to unlock potential and creativity throughout all areas of your life when experienced as a positive, high vibrational expression. By selectively choosing your partners and opening yourself physically, mentally, and emotionally, you unleash life-changing possibilities through the sacral chakra.

There is no such thing as casual sex. Although the physical act leaves the ego feeling temporarily satisfied, there are lingering effects left long past getting dressed. All the energies of emotional traumas and wounds you each subconsciously hold are transferred between partners. Doubt, insecurities, fear, guilt, abandonment, attachment, and so many more lower vibrational energies are unknowingly transmitted and retained for future transference. The good and the bad, the high and low vibrational energies are all exchanged during sex. Protecting yourself extends beyond physical, but to emotional and energetic.

Vampires

Not the type you see in movies that go around biting the necks of victims and drinking their blood, but energy vampires. The people in this category feed off your strong, positive, and radiant high vibrational energy. They are stealing from you. Taking your good attitude, uplifting emotions, and inner calmness, leaving you with low vibrational energies of feeling exhausted, irritated, tired, or drained after being around them.

Beware, often those with a lot of light and high vibrational energy attract those with great darkness because they are like a moth to a flame. The allure and temptation are too much to resist. Avoid these types of people at all costs. Energy vampires are draining you of your life force, and most valuable asset, your energy.

Narcissists and Internet Trolls

The prevalence of social media in our society has provided many delightful moments to share lives, perspectives, and gifts with the world. But where there are those with high vibrational energy and lights shining brightly, there are those who want to steal the spotlight and redirect attention toward themselves. Although everyone has a right to express their opinions, people must learn to accept and discuss instead of attacking and putting down.

Narcissists and internet trolls are selfish and arrogant people who cannot empathize. While likely experiencing undetected cognitive dissonance, they like to point out what is wrong rather than right and turn the blame onto others. They resist change and are sensitive to criticism and disagreements, although they would argue otherwise. Through comments and memes, they oppress, torment, and criticize. These people hold traumas and very low vibrational energy.

You cannot completely avoid or control narcissists and internet trolls. But you can set boundaries, protect your energy, and rise above responding or engaging. It is best practice to limit in-person interactions and unfriend or block someone behaving this way online, regardless of your relationship, as preventing low vibrational interactions is the healthiest thing to do.

If you recognize you may be one to respond negatively to something you see or read, I recommend not responding at all. Like Thumper recalls his mama saying in the beloved Disney children's classic, Bambi, "If you can't say something nice, don't say nothing at all." Instead of being a narcissist or internet troll, stop and recognize the feeling that arose within you. Then determine what needs to be healed inside you that made you want to react any way other than positively.

Personal Connection to Protecting Energy

Since I was a child, I never understood why I would tear up when I walked into a place like Disneyland, which should bring feelings of elation, intense joy, and unprecedented happiness. But hidden behind the smile on the outside were vast emotions absorbed from the collective sharing the experience. It is overwhelming when so much energy floods my senses. Through my awakening and understanding of energy, I am learning how to engage protective boundaries to limit exchanges of energies when going out in public places.

Reflection Section

Pause and reflect on protecting your energy. Can you identify some people in your life stealing your high vibrational energy? Are there places or situations you encounter that you need to take precautions? What changes can you make to protect your most valuable asset?

_____

_____

_____

_____

_____

_____

_____

_____

Protecting oneself from energies begins with valuing yourself above others, listening to your feelings, and being aware of situations and people attempting to steal your high vibrational energy. This awareness within you provides conscious recognition of threats to one's energy and allows for a choice to permit the flow of energy, transform it, or block it altogether.

Although relationships are essential, please recognize the closer you are to someone, the more vulnerable you are to transferring or unknowingly giving away your energy to them. Avoiding people pleasing and sacrificing yourself trying to make others happy retains your energy and power. It is not your responsibility to make someone happy; if they learn to follow their Magical Breadcrumbs, their happiness will also be revealed.

Higher Power Energies

Whether you choose to engage or not is your choice, but the energies of other souls surround us all the time. The light energies are positive and uplifting, like angels, spirit guides, and loved ones who have passed, are responsible for guiding you and sending you Magical Breadcrumbs. They are positive, can be trusted, and await your invitation to join you on your journey. But beware; there are also negative dark energies, and your abilities can attract both. It is about choice, intention, and action. Using your gifts of resonance and intuition allows you to decipher between the two and determine the decisions in alignment with your highest path and destiny. Do not let religious beliefs falsely lead you to think this is the occult or acting against God's word. Tapping into the energies aligned with your ego and soul's desires is when Magical Breadcrumbs arise, and manifestations and intentions materialize.

Personal Connection with Higher Power Energies

My connection to higher power energies has been a gradual realization throughout my life. Since I was a child, I had a deep inner knowing that peaceful, protective energies accompanied me I could not see. But it was not until many years later I realized people did not just die and go to Heaven when I saw my grandmother visit my infant son shortly after her passing. My awakening brought new spiritual intelligence and spiritual sight, confirming what I had always known in my heart. I now explicitly call upon my spirit team and all high vibrational energies for guidance and direction and the receipt of Magical Breadcrumbs. This ensures my powers are used for pure and good intentions.

Pause and reflect on your thoughts on higher vibrational energies. There are many underlying beliefs here that you may have yet to recognize. Do you believe in them? Why or why not? How do you feel about dark and light energies surrounding you? Do you believe in one over another? Keep digging until you find your answers.

_____

_____

_____

_____

_____

_____

_____

_____

Although angels are usually depicted as peaceful, it is crucial to recognize angels are warriors. They are fighting for your path to what is in alignment with your highest good and destiny. And although the actions may cause pain or leave collateral damage to an ego existence, they can be called upon to lead, guide, show, teach, tell, and protect you from dark and negative energies. Opening yourself to their existence and learning to communicate with them through Magical Breadcrumbs opens the doors to unlimited possibilities and abundance.

Restless Soul Syndrome (RSS)

When you find yourself feeling irritable and unfulfilled for an unknown reason, Restless Soul Syndrome may be to blame. From the outside, everything in your life looks as if it is going according to plan, but you cannot quite put your finger on what's wrong. You feel like something is missing or lacking, an overall restlessness, unhappiness, or boredom that seems unfounded yet overwhelming. This is caused by an imbalance of energies between the ego and soul, where lifestyle and choices have been too heavily controlled and weighted onto the materialistic side of life.

Your feelings are Magical Breadcrumbs from your soul persuading and urging you to make choices that make your higher self and inner child happy. Expressing creativity and finding methods to express your true self are the keys to rectifying this imbalance. Permit yourself to try new things that ignite your excitement and passion for life. It is never too late to balance your energies; just follow the Magical Breadcrumbs!

Personal Connection with Restless Soul Syndrome

Struggling with RSS is something I face regularly as I learn how to integrate my awakening self into my existing life. Choosing to live both an ego and soul existence creates a disconnect, resulting in the restlessness of my soul. Unexpectedly, I will feel as if something is missing, like I need to move, a restlessness that goes beyond just being bored. Sometimes, it is downright relentless and overwhelming, while other times are just a gentle tug. I find relief by following my Magical Breadcrumbs, spending time with my Twin Flame, acting toward my mission and purpose, expressing creativity, or socializing with others who share my spiritual views and experiences.

Reflection Section

Pause and reflect on Restless Soul Syndrome. Have you experienced a time you can relate to this feeling? Perhaps it is only occasional, or you thought it was a midlife crisis, but you felt pulled to something unknown. How do you feel knowing this was your soul and inner child crying out for attention, begging you to make a change and listen to your true heart's desires? What can you do to relieve the discomfort when you experience it again?

_____

_____

_____

_____

_____

_____

Beware! Attempting to escape RSS through alcohol, drugs, or sex will only provide temporary relief. Although mind-altering experiences relax the part of you that tries to control everything, returning you naturally to more of a flow state, it is only temporary. Once the effects wear off, the RSS returns even more relentlessly than before, potentially creating a vicious cycle of addiction. Instead, incorporate things you are naturally drawn to or that make you happy. The only way to eliminate Restless Soul Syndrome is to follow your Magical Breadcrumbs, fully embrace your soul, and allow it to lead you through life.

Chapter 8

Divine Magic

Although all people have free will, Source has the ultimate power and control over the Universe, and all that inhabits it. To ensure the divine design is followed, Source uses several standard tools to direct people into making free-will choices pointing toward their highest good and ultimate destiny, including timing, intervention, and opportunities. If you look closely as they happen, you will see each is filled with your Magical Breadcrumbs.

Honoring Divine Timing

Behind Magical Breadcrumbs, there is an invisible timeline that cannot be forced or rushed. Regardless of how hard you try or push for something, things happen to keep you on your path or move you onto a new one that is in the highest alignment of your destiny. When the Universe says it's time for something, it happens. Uncontrollable by people, perceived as positive or negative, look out, here it comes! Magic happens when you least expect it!

The deliverance of divine timing can feel inconvenient, hurtful, and unnecessary, or like relief and delight to the ego, but there is a higher purpose determined by factors of soul growth that cannot be seen. Only Source knows when the time is right. Sometimes, what our egos have worked so hard for is brushed aside by divine timing to allow something dramatic to happen, aligning us with our destiny. It is not necessarily bad, but the cycle's ending allows for a new beginning aligning with your soul. Time, as people measure it, does not exist in the Universe.

The concept of time, as people know it, imprisons, regulates, and controls us. Think about how often you check the clock every day to see what time it is or look at a calendar to see how many days until something arrives: a day off work, a birthday, an anniversary, a holiday, how long until your vacation or retirement we are always asking ourselves, how long? You're always waiting for the time to tell you when to do whatever comes next. You probably even wake to an alarm clock interrupting valuable connections to healing and replenishing your body. Time, when misused, steals priceless now moments by interrupting the natural flow, blocking your Magical Breadcrumbs.

I know it is extreme and impossible to give up the sense of time altogether. But consider that no matter what you do, or don't do, if it is the greater will of the Universe, it will happen regardless, so only live by the limitations of clocks and calendars when necessary to clear the path for the arrival of your Magical Breadcrumbs sooner.

Try this next time your schedule allows. Do not plan any appointments or set any alarms or timers. Avoid looking at anything indicating time. When you free yourself from expectations and judgments and allow your heart to gravitate toward what you do, you will feel joy because you naturally engage in things you enjoy. The longer you try this experiment, the more remarkable the transformation. I strongly encourage you to journal during this experience because it will be life-altering if you truly let go of time's imprisonments and observe your natural tendencies. These natural tendencies are Magical Breadcrumbs.

Where and how we live are factors of our attitudes towards time. Those of us in large cities are accustomed to days of hustle and bustle, being caught up in doing and always hurrying from one place to the next, too busy to stop and smell the roses. This contrasts those living lifestyles where 'coastal time' is practiced, and people use the clock as a tool rather than a rule. There, people tend to be more relaxed about appointments and obligations, and they relate more freely to one another and their surroundings. Societal programming feeds into the illusions through time and how we utilize it. For years, I have said we will look back on this period in history and remember there was never enough time. It is not because there is insufficient time, but we are focused on the wrong things that unnecessarily consume our time.

Personal Connection to Divine Timing

On Christmas morning, at the age of 28, I was gently woken by a tug on my left shoulder. Without moving, I opened my eyes and looked around the room. Soft sunlight was illuminating the space, but the air appeared hazy. I could see my husband and our pets all sleeping soundly beside me. I heard only silence. And then a gentle angelic voice said, "Go take a pregnancy test." For reasons I cannot explain, I trusted the directives. I quietly crept down the hall and did as I was told, and to my surprise, before I even finished washing my hands, the test revealed a positive result.

Although the news was not unexpected, the pregnancy came as a surprise, as I hadn't been able to conceive. This experience reinforced my belief that if it is meant to be, it will be, but it was also my first experience with clairaudience and clairsentience. Source had delivered all these gifts wrapped up in divine timing.

My oldest son was born the following summer and holds the middle name Destin, as I believe he was my destiny.

Reflection Section

Pause and reflect on how you feel about divine timing. Can you recall something unexpected that happened at a point in your life you could chalk up to divine timing? What happened? Can you see how it impacted the course of your journey? How does it make you feel now as you recognize it was Source delivering in divine timing and one of your Magical Breadcrumbs?

_____

_____

_____

_____

_____

_____

_____

_____

Time influences our lives in almost every conceivable way. Not only dictating when we need to do something or must be somewhere, but the false beliefs lying invisibly behind times when your ego chooses a responsibility over something that fulfills you deeper. When you pass up opportunities or cut experiences short that you enjoy because you feel time constrains you, you act opposite to your soul's desires and block the rising of Magical Breadcrumbs and your natural tendencies to experience joy and happiness.

Divine Intervention

Divine intervention arises when your actions and free-will choices are not currently in alignment with your highest destiny, are not a lesson needing to be learned, or are harmful or potentially destructive. Divine intervention is when

Source stands in the way, redirects, removes, or prevents something from happening; it is also commonly called fate.

Although divine intervention is often viewed or felt as a punishment, disappointment, or rejection, this is the Universe's way of protecting you or stopping you from making untimely choices and decisions that will lead to something not meant for you. Think about it as if some of the Universe's greatest gifts are unfulfilled prayers. It is not that they are not heard; it is that they are not in alignment with your highest potential and ultimate destiny,

Personal Connection to Divine Intervention

I accredit divine intervention for leading me to continue the Twin Flame journey after we were separated by 1200 miles. I was happily beginning a new chapter in my life, rebuilding my family in a new city with fond memories of my time with him. Then divine intervention stepped in and led me back into his arms and onto my path to awakening. It was then I discovered that time does not exist in souls. Months had passed since our last time together, yet immediately, it was as though we had never parted. Our egos immediately reacted submissively, and our souls led us to the next Magical Breadcrumb! You would not be reading this book if divine intervention had not occurred.

Reflection Section

Pause and reflect on how you feel about divine intervention. Can you recall a time when you were making poor decisions or headed down a path of self-destruction, and something unexpected happened to turn your life around? Or when something seemed impossible or too good to be true, yet it happened? Or did a prayer you made not turn out how you had hoped? How does it make you feel now that you recognize it was divine intervention and a Magical Breadcrumb?

_____

_____

_____

_____

_____

_____

_____

_____

When things do not turn out as you had thought, hoped, or planned, look at the situation, see the positives in the outcome, and know something better is waiting for you down another path. Just open your heart and watch for the signs invisibly leading you. It's never too late to turn your life around; follow your Magical Breadcrumbs and claim your right to happiness.

Divine Opportunities

The key to life is experiencing as much as you can! Say yes to opportunities, even when fear or doubt makes you want to say no, and then take everything in within every moment. Incorporate all your senses. See what surrounds you, hear the sounds nearby, touch everything you can get your hands on, taste the flavors within the experience on your tongue, and smell the aromas. Let go of judgments and expectations. Don't try to control the outcome. Just let the experiences happen. Unbelievable things occur when you do. This is called being in the now moment or present. Think of every now moment as a gift to unwrap all the possibilities Source gives you.

Every experience is about feeling. Truly allowing yourself to take in the moments of life and recognizing how they make you feel. Some are high vibrations and make you feel on top of the world, while others are low vibrations and raise negative emotions. You are safe to feel them all. Experience them and then sit with the feelings and let those feelings permeate your heart. It is those feelings that guide you toward your Magical Breadcrumbs.

Feelings are guidelines for making choices. Once you have experienced and felt an opportunity, you can choose if you will engage in the experience again or use it as an opportunity to learn and not repeat it. Whatever you choose, it is your life and your choice, but know those experiences that provide happiness and joy align with who you are at a soul level. And following them allows the breadcrumbs to fall into place, leading you to more soul-alignment experiences and opportunities.

Personal Connection to Divine Opportunities

I was blessed with the divine opportunities to conceive, carry, and deliver two healthy boys. Although both my pregnancies were high-risk and emotional rollercoasters, I was filled with love, hope, and gratitude as I nurtured my babies, feeling more radiant than ever. Even though I faced many scary times along the way, I treasured every moment.

Seeing their little faces on the ultrasound filled me with awe and joy at the miracles of creation. Feeling them kicking in my ever-expanding belly made me wonder how they could fit in there; every pungent smell made me queasy, and the pregnancy cravings seemed never-ending. But once in my arms, the touch of their soft skin nestled against my chest filled my heart with boundless love. I allowed myself to absorb all the experiences and emotions without succumbing to fear and the unknown and just basked in the miracles of motherhood.

Reflection Section

Pause and reflect on a memory tied to at least one of your senses. What made the experience so memorable? Maybe the smell of your grandmother's cookies in the oven, the sight of a childhood toy, the touch of a lover's hands, the taste of mom's cooking, or the feeling of joy playing at the park? Or perhaps something else memorable to you. Can you see now where these were divine opportunities etched into your heart forever?

_____

_____

_____

_____

_____

_____

_____

_____

Be aware that opportunities within now moments are often missed when focusing on our smartphones. Seeing and experiencing through the lens of the camera on a device provides a barrier that detracts your attention and your capabilities to absorb all your senses and recognize Magical Breadcrumbs. So, put down your phone and rely on your soul to give you the most precious memories.

Chapter 9

Mind-Blowing Concepts

Going with the Flow

Have you ever heard someone say, "Just go with the flow," or perhaps you have solicited this advice to others? It means to go along with instead of against; it is the opposite of controlling. The concept of flow can be easily recognized and related to by imagining a hallway filled with people; your movement is easier if you walk in the same direction as everyone else. However, if you walk toward other people, you will likely encounter congestion, restriction, and difficulty moving.

Think of the flow of water. Natural elements dictate which way the water runs in oceans, lakes, streams, and rivers. You may be surprised to hear running water is a Magical Breadcrumb in plain sight for everyone to see. Being near running water naturally transforms your body into a flow state. This is why many people find running water peaceful and tranquil, choosing to see and listen to it to relax or heal. It is an example of how life is supposed to be. Just like the seasons change, the flowers know when to bloom, and trees know when to lose their leaves; flow happens naturally and without the control of anyone. When man intervenes and tries to control the flow of nature, things become complicated and result in unnatural and undesired results.

The flow within one's life is not always easy to recognize. Although we tend to think of needing to go with the flow occasionally, it is a concept that should be incorporated into our daily lives. The flow of one's life indicates following what is led by your soul rather than your ego. To honor your spark, your ego and soul should flow together instead of moving against one another. When both are headed in the same direction, one experiences peace, joy, and happiness.

To go with the flow of your soul, you must let go of control. As humans with egos, we like to control outcomes. Many people mistakenly think control is powerful, and society often falsely attributes success to one's control over their life. While making plans and goals and working hard toward them likely makes us feel competent and accomplished, it can also look like missed opportunities and unnecessary self-induced stress trying to get things done against the flow. Although, in the end, utilizing control will probably result in the ego's desired outcome, a better choice is setting an intention and allowing the Universe to provide.

Personal Connection to Going with the Flow

For years leading up to this moment, at least a million little Magical Breadcrumbs were arising, leading to the chance encounter with my Twin Flame that changed my life forever. If I hadn't gone with the flow through career changes and life situations, I wouldn't have had the opportunities I had at that time, and this story would undoubtedly be different. However, because it was my destiny, the Universe would have rearranged circumstances and united us in another way.

Intention

Going with the flow is essential when setting intentions. Intention is something you have in mind that originated in your heart and soul. When one's mind recognizes a dream, wish, or desire in the heart stemming from the soul's desires, an opportunity for intention arises. Our human minds and egos often want action immediately, but with the case of intentions, the Universe will decide when it is time for it to become a reality, often revealing results better than our minds could have ever imagined.

Think of intention as an in-specific dream. You recognize your want and you may act towards it, but you release attachment from any preconceived outcome of how it will happen or end up. Let go and believe that if it's meant to be, it will be. Let the Universe complete and fulfill your heart's desire.

Personal Connection to Flow and Intention

For as long as I can remember, my husband and I have said someday we wanted to grow old in a house with a three-car garage, enough property for an RV, and a park nearby with just enough room for our family, but not too much to maintain. We didn't try to control when, where, or how it would happen. We just reinforced the thoughts over the years and fostered the dream. We now live in the exact house we intended, and it's better than we could have ever imagined. And it happened when we thought we were not yet ready to buy, and it was in a neighborhood we had not considered. The Universe delivered our intention beyond our expectations.

Manifestation

Manifestation is the ability to achieve your hopes and dreams radiating through your mind and heart space. When one's ego and soul align, one is in flow and connected to the Universe; they can create through the Law of Attraction.

The Law of Attraction is about alignment. Think about a magnet. When your energy smoothly flows between your soul and ego life, your desires are drawn effortlessly into the energetic field. It is a mindset and perception, like optimism versus pessimism. When one thinks positively, positive things occur, as opposed to when one thinks negatively, and negative results arise. Your thoughts and actions attract.

Just as each of us is unique, we may attempt to manifest differently. There are countless methods to attract tangible things into our lives: saying affirmations, setting intentions, creating vision boards, and through rituals with moon cycles; your creativity only limits the list of possibilities. A manifestation is not a recipe that must be followed precisely, but a continuity between the space within you where the desire originated and one's alignment within and with Source. It is the unison of thoughts and actions that attract like magnets.

Here are a few essential things to remember about manifestation:

1. Your desire must completely align throughout your ego and soul.
2. Attempts to control the outcome must be resisted; release expectations and go with the flow.
3. Drop any associated timelines; the Universe does not operate on the human concept of time and will deliver in divine timing.

If manifestation is not working, it is because there is a disconnection within you. Perhaps it is in one's level of faith, an alignment between ego and soul, an underlying controlling mechanism, an unrecognized false belief, or the lack of showing gratitude. Critically analyze each of these areas to identify potential blocks. Everyone can manifest, especially when you base them upon your Magical Breadcrumbs.

Personal Connection with Manifestation

This book is my manifestation. I always thought of writing something, but never knew what it would be or if it would come to fruition. It was simply a dream within my heart. Although I included it in my bucket list and wrote it into a journal entry, it was not until my ego dream united with my soul's purpose that the Universe delivered.

Despite several beginnings, changing storylines, and timeline adjustments, I did not allow myself to become discouraged. I kept my faith and went with the flow, knowing it would be if it were meant to be, and now here it is, in your hands; the book I manifested in what I consider divine perfection.

Pause and reflect on the amount of control you exhibit in your life. Are you the type to plan everything from start to finish, or do you tend to go with the flow and be more spontaneous? What changes can you make to allow more flow in your life? How can you see this benefiting you?

_____

_____

_____

_____

_____

_____

_____

_____

When you are in flow, you naturally and effortlessly follow Magical Breadcrumbs, and when you follow the Magical Breadcrumbs, more appear. But beware, the ego quickly and easily sabotages the divine plan through tendencies to control what is flowing. And sometimes, when that happens, divine timing and divine intervention intervene and force one to make decisions, moving them toward flowing with Source's plan.

The key to determining if you are genuinely intending/ manifesting or controlling is effort. If it requires effort from you to make it happen, you are controlling it. And through control, we allow unrecognized breadcrumbs to pass us by!

Change

Everything changes. Seasons, routines, circumstances, relationships, surroundings, evolving, and changing are embedded in every part of the flow of life. A newborn growing into an infant, then a toddler, then a preschooler, an adolescent, and a teenager are welcomed, as they are anticipated changes, and people know what to expect. But beliefs of the same expectations of personal evolvement cease for adults. Change is an inevitable part of life and should be looked forward to as an opportunity for growth and expansion at every age. Changes occur effortlessly when one is in flow and integrates them into life smoothly.

Change is about becoming different, from slight to extreme. Although it sounds simple enough, it is when the complexity of human emotions and the implications of a change are realized that surrounding circumstances must also evolve, and people and their feelings must be recognized. Existing relationships operate on developed patterns established on predictability. People find comfort in knowing how someone will act or react and what actions and reactions are likely to come next. The one making or experiencing the changes has all the control, while those intimately connected are left to adapt and adjust. Showing grace, empathy, compassion, and patience for yourself and all involved is essential for smooth transitions.

Sometimes, change feels refreshing and positive, but more often, it feels negative, daunting, and scary because it is unknown what will be on the other side of the change. We can see what we have now and what we stand to lose, but we cannot measure the unknown. What we have to gain is often incomprehensible, leading to uneasiness and insecurity within the one changing and those involved.

Change within and to one person alters the dynamics of existing relationships, causing additional changes to occur. Minor or infrequent changes with time to adjust between are usually easier to adapt to than significant or sequential ones. It is common for cognitive dissonance to arise here when beliefs interfere with making new life choices or changing one's mind about something, and fear often arises of criticism or abandonment of loved ones when a decision for something new is made. Remember, no one can stay the same throughout their entire lives.

One's attitude determines the outcome. A positive mindset and perspective show the bright side, the silver lining. So, look at the positive effects of change, show yourself grace, and release the guilt of the undesired implications. Change brings newness and excitement. Change allows one to expand by experiencing new things, developing new perspectives, and bringing new possibilities.

Personal Connection to Change

The year I met my Twin Flame started terrifically. My husband and I celebrated our twentieth wedding anniversary by taking the kids on a tropical vacation. Our family was healthy, work was going well for my husband and me, and we were happy and in love. I thought life couldn't get any better. Boy, was I wrong. I met my Twin Flame, and everything about me began changing from the inside out. But my changes started a chain reaction on those closest to me, including my children and husband. Although there is a distinct line between the before me and the now me, I would change nothing about my journey. I embrace the changes, knowing they are for my highest good and ultimate destiny.

Reflection Section

Pause and reflect on your feelings revolving around change. How do you typically react to changes at work or home, with friends or family? What was a change in your life that was welcomed? What would be one forbidden change and why? How does it make you feel knowing change is natural?

_____

_____

_____

_____

_____

_____

_____

_____

Find comfort knowing that Magical Breadcrumbs will guide you through times of change. Learning to use them to lead you relieves pressure and stress associated with thoughts of making wrong decisions as they are providing your movement in the right direction.

Releasing

Probably the single hardest concept for our egos to grasp is releasing. Releasing what no longer serves us, or what has served its purpose, and letting go. Releasing goes hand-in-hand with going with the flow and change. The more you go with the flow, welcome changes, and gracefully release what's not meant for you, the more Magical Breadcrumbs will arise, leading you toward joy, happiness, and your highest good.

Releasing can apply to someone and something, most commonly a relationship or attachment. A marriage, a partnership, a job, an addiction, a behavior, a friendship. Anything you recognize as no longer aligning with who you are or the direction you are headed in life. Releasing requires recognizing the change in the relationship, followed by conscious and intentful actions of acknowledging feelings, expressing honesty, speaking one's truth, and the ego release of attachments and expectations. While simultaneously overcoming false beliefs that one is giving up or giving in, breaking promises, or losing and the feelings related, including hurt, guilt, disappointment, sadness, rejection, and abandonment. Releasing forces everyone involved to face changes.

To release, one must be grateful. Embrace the purpose and past beauty of the situation, regardless of the evolving dynamics of life and existing relationships. Then, show grace, compassion, empathy, and strength for yourself and others as you transition. Remember, it is not always about you, and although you believe you are doing the right thing by holding onto a situation according to your ego or cultural beliefs, the Universe may be making room for an opportunity to arise or align someone else for their highest good. Releasing is selfless and allows moving forward and limitless possibilities for everyone involved, and it restores and returns personal power.

Do not underestimate the power of the beliefs behind your hesitation to release. Remember, the thoughts or opinions of others are not your concern, as what may be right for your life may not be for another. This could apply to how relationships look to society. There is no one-size-fits-all functional, loving relationship. It's about support, communication, and harmonious living that are essential, and getting there is as unique as each of us.

Releasing may be karmic. Attempt to recognize patterns between situations. If you fail to act toward releasing, patterns will continue to surface, showing one the healing and action required until one has no other option but to address the situation and make a different choice. If one chooses not to release willingly and gracefully what is no longer in their alignment, the Universe will continue to show you the pattern until you are forced to let go.

Personal Connection to Releasing

Spiritually awakening changed everything for me, including the patterns of my marriage. My husband and I were forced to face the decision to stay together or divorce. We released what was to allow what will be to blossom. We are grateful for our family and the memories we share from years together. But, releasing the shadows, expectations, and beliefs surrounding our relationship allowed for a new beginning. Although it was an emotionally painstaking process requiring compassion, we made decisions that allowed our relationship to be renewed.

Reflection Section

Pause and reflect on a time when you released something or someone. It might look like a breakup with a partner, quitting a job, or severing a friendship. How did it make you feel at the time and today? Now stop and think about when someone else released you. Did you get fired, or did someone break up with you? Reflect on the emotions then and now. Is there a situation in your life currently that you need to consider releasing?

_____

_____

_____

_____

_____

_____

_____

_____

Sometimes, you must release things attached to your ego self to allow your soul to soar to its greatest height. Just listen to your heart, follow the Magical Breadcrumbs, and release the guilt that may attempt to creep in.

Letting Go

You are not alone. We all torture ourselves by holding on to the past and things that have happened. Letting images and memories play out like a movie in our minds a million times. We hope that somehow, we could change what happened or recognize a piece of vital information we missed before that would make us feel better. What has happened is in the past, and the past cannot be changed no matter how many times you rehash it over and over. But the part of you here now needs to heal whatever it holds onto and let go to find peace within.

Things happen how they are meant to, which is difficult for our ego mind to comprehend when it wants to control everything. Letting go applies to emotions that arise when relationships end and when people die.

You have probably heard the ancient proverb, 'Time heals all wounds.' When intense emotions are involved, the need to recognize and release them is essential, but truly, it is the passing of time that can change perspectives and circumstances and lessen associated emotions. However, anyone obsessing over a situation should consider the assistance of a licensed therapist who can offer support through the healing process.

The acronym 'Let Go' can help you remember the steps of working through the release and letting go process.

- **L-** Let the associated emotions arise. The feelings you experience are specific to you. Recognize that others going through similar situations likely have different emotions surrounding them, and do not assume you know how someone feels.
- **E-** Experience the arising emotions. Do not stop yourself from feeling the way you do. Instead, acknowledge. You can feel any emotion, and no one can tell you otherwise. Allow yourself to feel all the emotions that arise: guilt, shame, doubt, fear, pain, sadness, abandonment, rejection, etc.
- **T-** Tell yourself what you need to hear and forgive yourself.
- **G-** Give yourself permission to let go of the attached low vibrations you identified and move on, holding onto only the highest vibrations of love, admiration, respect, and appreciation.
- **O-** Open the doors of opportunity to reestablish connections with people in your life. Our hearts are made to love; sometimes, loss closes our hearts as protection in fear of another loss. But this defense mechanism can steal future joy and happiness.

When you are clear on the emotions that are arising and holding you back from moving on, let go of them. Go outside in the sunshine, look toward the sky, say each emotion and what comes to your heart, and visualize watching each feeling drift off in a bubble into the sky, going higher and higher for as long as you can see it. And when it is out of your sight, you have let it go, releasing it and making room for newness to enter your life—repeat the process through all emotions. Now, have faith that it's all part of the bigger picture and accept that things happen. It is what it is, and it was meant to be this way. You have cleared a new path for Magical Breadcrumbs.

Death

Letting go is especially difficult to understand when tragic accidents happen, or death occurs unexpectedly. Understand it is likely a soul contract has been fulfilled and when that happens, the human body is released, and the soul returns to Source. No one can prevent this from happening, and no matter what you had done differently, the outcome would have been the same. Accept that you cannot change what happened and forgive yourself and others involved.

Recognize just as our connections with faith are unique, following the loss of a loved one, we each need support from those remaining in our lives in a specific way that only we know. People closest to us will often become distant after tragedy strikes because they are uncertain of how to act or what to say; do not make the mistake of thinking they are insensitive or uncaring. You must tell them what you need and expect from them. Letting go of these connections without communicating stifles your recovery and healing, resulting in further losses and trauma.

Letting go of someone who has passed is not forgetting them. It's about remembering the beauty of the gift they brought to your life. Being thankful and grateful for the opportunity to know them, the time you had together, their impact on you, and the memories you treasure. They may be physically gone, but the bond you share lives on forever.

Physical passing from life to death opens new opportunities for connection. Death frees the soul, and it becomes unconfined by the limitations it had within its body. Although your relationship does not look like it used to, their love still surrounds you. When you realize your ability to tap into your intuition and heart to feel their presence and recognize

Magical Breadcrumbs, emotions alchemize from low vibrational to high vibrational, and distance is transcended. You are creating a refreshing new beginning.

Personal Connection to Letting Go

For almost my entire life, I was blessed to have a close relationship with a brother and his wife, whom I considered my sister. I'd never imagined a day when we would not celebrate holidays and special events together, much less a week without talking. But that all changed over a decade ago when a conflict arose unexpectedly based on varying perceptions of actions, and underlying beliefs surfaced. Despite attempts to resolve this, irreversible damage was done on that fateful day that changed the family dynamics and created a division.

The issue that led to the conflict is not the part that needs to be revealed here. We simply had two different perspectives on a situation leading to an impasse. Neither right nor wrong, just unable to move past the intense emotions to reveal a resolution.

Betrayal, disappointment, and distrust arose for me. The story that repeatedly played in my mind was the length of time these thoughts and feelings had been stirring, and if they were pretending all along to care. I cried countless tears over it until I remembered everything happens for a reason.

I choose to be grateful for the years we had together, and I recognize our relationship had to be severed for me to stand outside their shadows and grow into the person I was meant to be. Choices I have made since the separation likely would not have happened if things had remained the same. My Magical Breadcrumbs led me to where I am, and to get there, I had to experience the pain and loss and learn how to let go.

Reflection Section

Pause and reflect on the concept of letting go. Have you ever been faced with having to let go of something or someone that was not your choice? How did you feel? Did any beliefs stand in your way of healing after? Can you recognize something in your life that it is time to let go of?

_____

_____

_____

_____

_____

_____

_____

_____

Letting go does not come easily. The need to let go is the ending of a relationship, a breaking up with the past. This is the part where you realize you cannot change what has happened and must release it to move forward. Find comfort in knowing Magical Breadcrumbs will arise to show you the way to go!

Balance

Most people think about balance only if doing physical activity, and many do not equate it to something essential in life. When you read the word balance, you may have even visualized an object balancing or a child on a bicycle or balance beam. But balance is not only one of the essential physical abilities within each of our lives; balance also contributes to personal satisfaction and internal peace and harmony.

Balance is about offsetting, which is essential to one's joy and happiness. Thinking about opposites is an easy way to recognize where balance may be lacking and then consciously introduce it into one's life. Work and play, activity and sedentary, sleep and wakefulness, healthy food and junk food, time with friends and time alone, giving and receiving, time with your children and time with your partner, inside and outside, the list goes on and on. When one activity or responsibility overshadows much of your life, an imbalance is created, leaving one feeling empty, irritable, or unhappy. Ensuring balance in one's life allows one to function in society and nurture one's soul essence.

But balancing goes beyond what you can physically see or do. There are fundamental elements to your soul requiring internal balance. Regardless of one's gender, within each of us, we have both feminine and masculine energies that require attention to remain balanced. The natural feminine energy traits are creative, nurturing, empathetic, and compassionate. In contrast, the natural masculine energy traits are progress, control, stability, protectiveness, applying logic and structure, accomplishing, and providing. Both the feminine and masculine energies are essential to creating harmony within that reflects outward into society and world order.

Culture and society have long been led by masculine energy. We see it all around us with the perceived necessity for progress and control. Our world has become too heavily weighted with masculine energies leading with their egos, but the tides are changing and feminine energies are rising. We are not abandoning masculine energies but balancing them to establish universal harmony where we create a society supporting one another and our Earth above all else. There, internal balance will radiate from each of us into the world around us.

Personal Connection to Balance

When my children were young, I was a very attentive mother. To me, motherhood is the single most important role in this life a woman has if she decides to have children. I spent every waking minute tending to their needs, preparing and providing everything I considered essential to them growing up healthy and happy. However, I realized a connection between my moods and happiness when I failed to balance time for self-care and developing personal relationships. After balancing time away to nurture myself, I was calm and refreshed, allowing myself to be more present and patient with them.

Reflection Section

Pause and reflect on how balance looks in your life. Can you see where you are doing something too much, creating an imbalance? Now, think about what you can introduce to offset the situation. You likely enjoy these things and wish you had more time to do them. Also, please consider it is highly likely you need to implement activities allowing for the traits associated with the opposite gender to be expressed. What can you implement today and this week to start balancing yourself? How do you think this will make you feel?

Although there are countless activities one can do to nurture either feminine or masculine energies, there is one place that supports both. Often, spending time in nature is a one-size-fits-all fix that offsets both too much time spent indoors and gender energy imbalances. Walking, hiking, camping, riding an all-terrain vehicle or bicycle, hunting, fishing, boating, geocaching, birdwatching, and anything else you can think of to enjoy the great outdoors is encouraged. Just surrounding and immersing yourself in nature naturally balances energies within, raises vibrations, restores harmony, and aligns one to receive Magical Breadcrumbs.

Stop

Stop and think about the mind-blowing concepts that integrate Magical Breadcrumbs into your life. Going with the flow, embracing change, releasing what no longer serves us, and letting go of stifling emotions are natural occurrences that may be difficult for our egos to do and comprehend, but are vital to our journey. It is through courageousness and balance that our energy is used effectively and efficiently, and we can appreciate where we have been and look forward to the future while knowing there is no more important moment than the one right in front of us.

Chapter 10

Unparalleled Empowerment

In this chapter, I share personal messages I have received directly from Source through clairaudience, which can help us all on our journeys. Although some people receive messages while awake, most of mine come to me in a space between being awake and asleep. Almost like a dream, it appears as if I am looking into infinity. Blackness slowly rotates horizontally, covered in sparkling yellow and white lights, like twinkling stars, and then I hear a soothing voice with a clear message.

These messages that I call downloads are bits of information used to guide, direct, or remind the receiver of important things and their connection with the Universe. Like data being downloaded into a computer, they improve function. For those of you with religious roots, you may notice the messages are uncannily similar to biblical verses. Although I have not tied them to the Bible, I encourage you to research and read up on them. They are Magical Breadcrumbs!

First Message

As the fuzziness and cloudiness started to lift and the sunshine swept across my face, I awakened from my dark night of the soul to the sweet sound of this message. The voice was as clear as if you and I were conversing. I was overwhelmed with love and felt supported by a force more significant than anything I can describe. I was amazed and bewildered.

"Everything you need is inside you."
Source

We were divinely created with everything we need inside of us. As infants and young children, we only knew ourselves as perfection and weren't afraid to shine our lights in the world. We cried when we were sad and yelled when we were angry. We danced to music and sang at the top of our lungs without concern about who was watching us or what they were thinking. We had open hearts and minds, eager to soak up all life offered. This is because, in early childhood, our souls exist harmoniously with our egos within our bodies, yet to be tainted by the human experience.

The veil between soul and ego was thin. Influences and those closest to us unknowingly introduced false beliefs and expectations that dimmed our lights and altered our behavior. As we grew, our actions became clouded with

154

acceptable and unacceptable societal programming, with rules for acting, thinking, and feeling. Emotions became something to bottle up, and we viewed them as bad or undesired, the opposite of our soul's desire. We became insecure, dependent, fearful, and lost sight of our innate abilities. During this period, our egos stepped up to protect us, creating a great divide between our souls and other people's beliefs and expectations based on untruths. But it's all an illusion. You have always been and will always be divinely perfect.

The perfect I refer to is how Source created you. There is only one of you, and you are uniquely you. You were made exactly the way you were intended. But, the idea of perfection created by the educational system and society is based on an ever-changing definition that varies between people and circumstances. What one views as perfect is subjective and specific to their beliefs and ideas and should not dictate your actions and reality. While you may think of it as someone's suggestion, it is not absolute. You have the power to decide what your perfect is.

Although the haze had not lifted from my mind, my eyes were puffy, and my vision was blurred; something inside me stirred. Then, I felt hopeful and powerful, and words of affirmation formed from my soul to my mind. I remembered my perfection.

I am smart.

I am funny.

I am beautiful.

I am strong.

I am courageous.

I am brave.

I am powerful.

I am sovereign.

I am worthy.

I am love.

I am light.

I am enough!

I encourage you to incorporate this mantra into your daily routine, and you will notice changes within yourself almost immediately. They are reminders of the warrior inside you. Recite them whenever you look in a mirror and feel defeated, anxious, or worried. Say them in the shower, in the car, walking, riding a bike, anywhere and anytime! Saying them out loud is best, but silently within your head also works. You are casting a spell on yourself to reclaim your personal power and remember your divine perfection. As a child, you were powerless and naïve. But no more! You have shed the false beliefs.

Earlier, I shared my connection to eliminate limiting beliefs introduced to me as a young child. When I was not allowed to go with my older siblings, the veil lifted for me, and my insecurities were created based on untruths. My ego stepped up to protect me from feeling left out, sad, angry, and not good enough. But one message from the Universe and I remembered I am whole, complete, and perfect by myself, just the way I am.

Reflection Section

Pause and reflect on the last time you were free to let yourself fully engage in the moment without a care in the world or a thought of what others were thinking of you. Can you even remember those times of innocence, or is it a memory of feeling awkward and judged that stands out? Now imagine what you will do differently when you remember you are smart, funny, beautiful, strong, courageous, brave, powerful, sovereign, and worthy.

_____

_____

_____

_____

_____

_____

_____

Each of our lives would be significantly different if we saw ourselves through the lens of perfection. When we remember we are all perfect, we realize we are equal and uniquely created to share our gifts—resulting in the return of personal power and the confidence to follow the Magical Breadcrumbs as they arise.

157

Second Message

"In all things, love."
Source

This message came as a reminder of how to act, regardless of the actions of others. Through the chaos that ensued after my Twin Flame encounter, I was shunned and criticized by some who judged me for my choices and my newfound spiritual path. This message revealed that each of us is responsible for putting love first.

If we were each asked to define love, it would vary based on our beliefs and experiences. Love is highly complex. We can love other people. We can love our jobs or our hobbies, ourselves, and our social organizations. We are free to love anything and everything. It is not just an emotion shared, but a respect and appreciation. Love is choosing the highest vibration in each situation.

To choose the highest vibrations, one must recognize polarities. Polarities are contradictory tendencies; they are opposites. Like health and sickness, happiness and sadness, anger and peace, love and fear, the list goes on and on, with one vibration lower than the other. To identify, look at the associated emotions and how they make one feel. The better you feel, the higher the vibration.

Showing ourselves and others grace is love. There are no mistakes but possibilities. Understand you are exactly where you are supposed to be, wherever you are. Undoubtedly, there have been lessons along the way, but accepting that you make what you feel is the best decision possible at the time puts love first.

Applying tolerance and acceptance of others' choices is love. It is unnecessary and unencouraged to agree with everyone all the time, but your response is expected to be one of love. Instead of making hurtful, demeaning, shaming, or humiliating comments, find a positive in every situation. Be grateful and thankful for them showing you a new idea or perspective. Do not fear what someone else has to say or a unique perspective; learn to love that they see things differently than you.

 **Reflection Section**

Pause and reflect on your feelings about love. Recognize that since you were born, beliefs have been instilled into you surrounding love. Do you associate love as a feeling within relationships or apply it as gratitude, unconditional acceptance, and appreciation? What can you start doing today to choose love in all things?

_____

_____

_____

_____

_____

_____

_____

A world where love prevails would be very different than it is now. People would be kind to one another and help each other regardless of the labels we each hold. Choices would favor people, living things, and the planet. We would be thriving instead of surviving.

 Third Message

"Carpe Diem"
Source

This was an unusual message I received at an unexpected time, but a much-needed reminder for most of us as we get caught up in day-to-day routines. In case you do not already know, The Roman poet Horace used the phrase "carpe diem," which means seize the day before you and do not worry so much about the future.

The past cannot be changed and should be honored as part of your journey. The memories and photographs remain proof of the times and moments gone by, but the distance behind you should not be dwelled upon, as no wishing, hoping, or reminiscing can change what has already happened.

The future has yet to be written. So many choices to be made and twists and turns to take throughout your life, leading you to your final destination. Overly planning and trying to control what comes tomorrow will only steal opportunities for today and lead to disappointment.

The real magic happens when you stay in the present moment to experience the gifts of what is being presented to you by the Universe. Not through a device lens or with a preoccupied mind, but with your own eyes and all your senses engaged to truly take in what the Universe is offering you right now. Embrace these moments with enthusiasm and an open heart as if they were your first encounter, and with appreciation it may be the last time you will ever experience it. It is these moments where memories are made, and Magical Breadcrumbs arise and lead you on your path toward your future.

Reflection Section

Pause and reflect on your thoughts on your relationship with the future. Are you the type to believe you are the creator of your destiny, or are you more of an I'll wait and see what happens kind of person? How does your view of the future impact your ability to live a carpe diem life and recognize and follow Magical Breadcrumbs?

_____

_____

_____

_____

_____

_____

_____

_____

"Eat, drink and be merry" is a proverb and a biblical reference reminding us of a similar message as Carpe diem. Follow your Magical Breadcrumbs and seize today and all this life's joys when you can, because tomorrow is not promised.

Fourth Message

"Sometimes you have to go back to heal."
Source

This message reminds us that although society pushes us to continue forward with life, sometimes the only way to resolve and heal is to go back. It can mean figuratively through memories or therapy or physically by rekindling a relationship or visiting and recalling a time with others. The repressed feelings, unfinished business, or lessons associated with the situation are why you must return to move forward. Time has allowed for lessening emotions and a more objective perspective, but it did not magically fix anything. To learn, heal, and grow, one must sometimes go back.

Society pushes us forward with celebrating birthdays. Depending on your culture, some even believe you are born at a year old or that you advance your age on the celebration of a new year. But inside, you are the same person today you were yesterday and every other day before, at every age of your life. Just because the sun rises on another day and the date on the calendar changes, it does not mean the old you disappears, that the past is erased, and you have a clean slate to start again. This life is a continuous journey.

Throughout each of our journeys, we experience life and learn lessons. While most are ordinary and do not require conscious thoughts or actions, some deserve greater attention. Apply the common expression, "the good, the bad, and the ugly," toward memories. Good times are remembered as happy with emotions like love, enjoyment, and laughter. The bad times were sad, unpleasant, or unfortunate. But the ugly are likely to include traumas with the most extreme emotions, like fear, rage, and anger.

The good times are recalled freely in trips down memory lane, allowing the emotions to rise again and feel grateful. The sad times are likely only occasionally discussed with close friends and family. But the traumas known as ugly times are unspeakable, unacceptable to others, or just so unbearable to think about, much less discuss. So, we try to bury and forget them. And our egos are there like soldiers protecting us from the feelings we felt when it occurred. But not addressing traumas does not eliminate them; it only suppresses and forces them to arise throughout the body as detachment, illnesses, and ailments. They are creating barriers between you and your Magical Breadcrumbs.

No matter how long ago something happened, there is no shame in returning to a situation or memory filled with unpleasantness, feeling the emotions that arise, and forgiving yourself or others involved. This heals unfinished business and allows you to see how a single situation dictated the course or actions you have taken in life since, providing an opportunity to change engrained behaviors and stop karmic cycles. Do not let your ego, pride, or anyone else tell you otherwise. We are each responsible for our own healing to move forward in life and engage in healthy relationships. Whether or not we realize it, failing to heal results in emotional barriers and dysfunctional communication patterns in future relationships. Protective walls are created, making one emotionally unavailable, separating us from the people and emotions we are here to experience, and obscuring our purpose and passions.

Reflection Section

Pause and reflect on the idea of receiving messages from Source. When guidance is offered through clairaudience, the receiver directly hears without interference from others' beliefs or interpretations. Can you see why these four messages were chosen to help you on your journey? Does one stand out from the rest that you feel guided to follow? Imagine how your life would change if you began receiving messages like these.

_____

_____

_____

_____

_____

_____

_____

_____

Chapter 11

Opening Doors to Abundance

Abundance is something we all desire but many of us see as slightly beyond our reach. Often, we fail to recognize what we already have and we unknowingly allow false limiting beliefs to tell us we are not worthy of more. Simply showing gratitude for what you have and believing you deserve begins aligning you to receive. But this is only the beginning.

Establishing healthy habits and routines and making conscious choices are also key components. When you incorporate small, consistent, positive practices into each day you are further attuning yourself to obtaining the joy, happiness, health, wealth and love you desire. The little things lead to big rewards, help you recognize your Magical Breadcrumbs, and suddenly doors of opportunity are opening. When you align your thoughts and feelings with abundance, you attract it.

Opening doors of abundance begins and ends with you. You can change your life and receive Magical Breadcrumbs leading to your heart's desires, starting with these 18 simple ways:

1. **Express Gratitude-** Before you even take your head off the pillow in the morning, think of at least three things you are thankful for and why. Being grateful for your health, loved ones, and surroundings set the day off to a positive start; and a grateful heart attracts more to be thankful for. Challenge yourself to see how many days in a row you can come up with different things. These feelings of gratitude are Magical Breadcrumbs.

2. **Unplug From Technology-** Set yourself time restrictions, boundaries, and limitations for engaging with technological devices. Limiting exposure increases your mood, benefits your health, and frees your mind. Addiction and dependence on our devices steal our focus, brainwash, and block our Magical Breadcrumbs.

3. **Respect Your Body-** Make choices about your body that honor both your ego and soul. Think beyond what you have heard about eating healthily, drinking water, and exercising. Expand your health requirements to include conscious choices about energies you allow into your field to maintain and lift your vibration and your ability to receive your Magical Breadcrumbs.

4. **Positivity in Media-** Carefully choose what you read and watch. Selectively view only those containing

positive and uplifting content and images. Doing this will separate you from negativity, programming, and limiting beliefs, allowing your Magical Breadcrumbs to flow more easily.

5. **Practice Intermittent Fasting**- Give your body spare time after processing what you consume, allowing it to focus on regenerating and maintaining health. It can be done at varying hours and times to accommodate your schedule, improving your sleep quality and overall health. Caring for your body invites Magical Breadcrumbs.

6. **Get Plenty of Rest**- Make sleep a priority, and don't overexert yourself. When you feel tired or like you need to rest, listen to the messages your body is sending and honor the vessel that allows you to experience life. Magical Breadcrumbs flow freely while your ego and body are resting.

7. **Go Outside**- Spend time outdoors every day; in the yard, visiting the park, walking during a lunch break, or hiking with friends changes our mindsets and moods. Look up and down and all around and appreciate the beauty of nature, while you breathe fresh air, see through unfiltered lighting, walk barefoot in the grass, and soak up natural Vitamin D. You will be amazed by the Magical Breadcrumbs surrounding you when you stop to smell the roses and hear the birds sing.

8. **Listen to Your Heart**- As you face decisions throughout your day, consult with your heart. Choices made from the heart, through your resonance, align with your greatest good. Close your eyes, put your hands to your heart, and visualize each choice individually until you realize where you feel a connection. Magical Breadcrumbs are hidden within resonance.

9. **Think Positively**- Train your mind to consider the positives in every situation before considering anything

else. When you think negatively, correct it with a thought of something you appreciate and then try thinking about the situation again from the attitude of gratitude. Remember the Law of Attraction; positivity attracts more positivity and Magical Breadcrumbs are positively leading you in the right direction.

10. **Put Yourself First-** When you nurture yourself and indulge in simple things that make you feel happy, you have more to give. Taking time for you recharges your energy and spirits. Even just a few minutes make a difference; love and appreciate yourself and what you do for others. Honoring yourself aligns you with receipt of Magical Breadcrumbs.

11. **Find Balance-** Each area of your life needs equal attention. Making time for the essentials and things you enjoy reflects in your mood, attitude, energy, and overall satisfaction with your life. Times you feel enjoyment align with your soul, follow the Magical Breadcrumbs to find them.

12. **Carpe Diem-** Be present in all that you do. Engage and enjoy yourself without any barriers, partake in every moment before you. Seizing the moments to connect with others opens you up to Magical Breadcrumbs.

13. **Openly Communicate-** Advocate for what you want and need to be happy. Developing proactive strategies, setting boundaries, and talking with others maintains your sovereignty. Besides, science shows you'll likely live longer if you don't keep things bottled up inside you. Open your throat chakra and speak your truth; your words line the way for your Magical Breadcrumbs to appear.

14. **Honor Your Emotions-** Emotions are intended to be embraced and felt. If you feel sad, share it; if you feel mad, express it appropriately; if you feel excited, show

it; and if you feel love or gratitude, say it. Remember our emotions and the ways we feel are Magical Breadcrumbs.

15. **Play-** Engage in activities not for purpose but for mere enjoyment. Have a sleepover, start a pillow fight, go outside and play in the dirt, build with blocks or Legos, play a game, paint, or draw. Do whatever makes you feel happy. Your inner child will love you for it and Magical Breadcrumbs will arise.

16. **Smile-** Your smile can change the world. It is a universal communication tool we all have and is available to give and receive freely. A single smile shows friendliness, can brighten someone's day, sends messages of being seen, appreciated, and accepted, and conveys joy and happiness. A smile is a Magical Breadcrumb.

17. **Listen to Frequencies-** Instead of listening to music, implement listening to frequencies while engaging in chores, working or sleeping. Frequencies can help you focus, be creative, heal, connect with Source, rest, and so much more. The brain absorbs them, allowing you to quiet the ego mind, raise your energetic vibrations and drift into a place of productive peace and being present, giving Magical Breadcrumbs a window of opportunity to be recognized.

18. **Nourish Your Soul-** Find a few minutes every day in quietness to bring peace and stillness to your mind. This allows disconnection from your ego to connect with your higher self and Source. Prioritizing time daily for meditation, prayer, deep breathing, yoga, or journaling will enable you to focus, perform, connect, and recognize Magical Breadcrumbs better throughout the day.

Reflection Section

Pause and reflect on the little recommended changes to open doors of abundance. Choose at least two and commit to doing them for the next 22 days to form habits. What changes do you hope to see in your day-to-day life by implementing them? Integrating little things in your days opens opportunities of abundance and aligns you with your Magical Breadcrumbs.

_____

_____

_____

_____

_____

_____

_____

_____

To receive Magical Breadcrumbs, you must align with the Universe's frequency. Like a song playing on the radio, if there is interference in the signal, the tune will not play clearly. With each little positive life change you implement; you are slowly tuning into the exact frequency to receive your messages.

Chapter 12

Daring to Reach Destiny

With every ending, there is a beautiful opportunity for a new beginning. As we near the end of this book, look back and be thankful for how far you have come in this life and everything that has led you to this moment. Be grateful for the people and the experiences that have made you who you are today; then, you can look forward to a life filled with abundance where you follow your inner guidance and the resonance within your heart and bravely move forward, daring to reach your destiny.

Rise Individually

Every second of every minute, every hour of every day, you have the power and the ability to make choices, gifts of opportunity to change your life and embrace your sovereignty. Let go of the past and any limitations or regrets you carry, as they do not define you. Recognize your thoughts are not confined to patterns, and regardless of the expectations of others, you are not bound to do things the same way you did in the past. Remember, change is the only constant in life. Be courageous, follow your faith, and trust in the divine plan.

Let go of control and follow your Magical Breadcrumbs; they reveal your path to destiny. Going with the flow gives you the freedom to grow and change naturally without approval from anyone. As cliché as it may sound, think of the caterpillar that turns into a butterfly. No one tells or grants permission for a caterpillar to form a chrysalis, allowing it to reinvent itself and come out completely different yet stunning. Be the butterfly! Be fearless of what comes next. Believe you are worthy of all the love and abundance that life offers, remember your perfection, and realize you are one amongst many rising at this time.

Rising Together

Recognize we live in a world of dualities where both beauty and darkness surround us every day, and although it seems that power, control, corruption, and violence are increasing, they are just being revealed. The time has come when we bravely face the effects of imbalanced masculine energies and allow those of the feminine to rise and lead us into a new world of balance where peace, love, and prosperity prevail. Look around you; those embracing these qualities are emerging. Be strong and supportive; embrace the possibilities and freedom this brings.

Be one who recognizes the similarities and embraces the differences amongst us. Have hope that our children can grow up in a world where no one needs to proclaim their lives matter or where laws are necessary to protect individual rights. Let the illusions dissolve that have been falsely created by those in positions of leadership that separate us and point out our differences. Everyone is equally worthy, and we each have the divine right to share our uniqueness, to be accepted and celebrated unconditionally for our soul's expression, where there are no superficial comparisons, competitions, or judging.

We are all interconnected and part of the culture of the Universe. Choosing remembrance of your divine perfection frees your soul's spark to shine brightly. Like a pebble thrown into a creek, you create a ripple effect on the waters around you, and those in your family, your community, and your culture begin changing too. Joining together empowers us to defeat the darkness by casting our lights onto the shadows, breaking them apart, and allowing those suppressed to rise.

"And the light shineth in darkness; and the darkness comprehended it not."
(John 1:5 KJV)

Personal Connection to Daring to Reach Destiny

Today, I hardly recognize myself as the woman I described in the first chapter. My entire perspective on life has changed. When the veils of deceit and distractions were lifted, I saw what really matters and realigned my thoughts and vision to those of greater purpose.

Once I believed in myself and the unseeable, I released the need to control and stopped resisting change and replaced them with flow. Those changes combined revealed a conversation of guidance between the Universe and me that I call Magical Breadcrumbs. When I am in flow, I am led to the people, places, and experiences I am destined for and the joy and happiness I desire.

Although I recognize that while I will still encounter challenges; and stumble along the way, I realize each misstep leads to a lesson and a moment of personal growth. I will show myself grace and remember there are no mistakes in life. There is nothing I cannot do or overcome; everything I need is inside me.

From now on, I intend to get it all right. I vow to lead a life aligned with my purpose and passion. I will follow my guidance to help others rise, and I will spend the rest of my life counting the times my breath is taken away while I dare to reach for my destiny and am fearless in following my Magical Breadcrumbs!

Reflection Section

Pause and reflect on how you feel about daring to reach your destiny. Are you just going through life as a victim of circumstances, or are you living a life of intention and purpose? If low vibrational energies arise in your reflections or you feel frustrated or dissatisfied with your life choices, it is time to break free from the illusions and rise individually and together.

_____

_____

_____

_____

_____

_____

_____

_____

Daring to reach your destiny is within your control. Free will allows you the opportunity to continue to be trapped within the rat race of life or consciously choose to rise above and recognize the abundance waiting for you. There are no second chances; once time has passed, it is gone, but it is not too late. Be brave and learn to balance your soul's desires within your life. The entire Universe is supporting you and waiting for you to ask for your Magical Breadcrumbs to lead you to endless joy and happiness.

Stop

Stop and think about the life waiting for you. A life where you are not alone in navigating through the obstacles but one where messages of guidance provide unparalleled empowerment that fills you with confidence and supports your sovereignty. One where you receive all the abundance you desire just because you shine your inner light brightly.

Now, little spark, stop and take a deep breath and smile; your path to destiny has been revealed, and it's waiting for you to take the next step.

**_Believe in yourself and believe in
the power of Magical Breadcrumbs._**

18 Key Takeaways

1- You are created in divine perfection!

2- Recognize you have an ego and a soul, and both have purpose and needs.

3- Follow your divine gifts of excitement, gut feelings, resonance, and passion.

4- Open your heart and mind to connect with the magic of the Universe.

5- Meet new people and build relationships.

6- Embrace and release all emotions as they arise and pass through you.

7- Experience each moment unfiltered.

8- Be aware of anyone that makes you feel fearful.

9- Consciously choose your beliefs.

10- Find your faith.

11- Go back to heal past traumas and reclaim your personal power.

12- Be aware of how energy influences you.

13- Let go of control and go with the flow.

14- Understand everything changes.

15- Release what no longer serves you and let go of what you cannot change.

16- Always show gratitude.

17- Abundance is within your reach.

18- Bravely pursue your Magical Breadcrumbs!

Top 5 Ways to Let Your Inner Light Shine!

1. Smile- A smile is the most universal gesture in the world. It costs nothing to give but provides a gift of acknowledgment, support, appreciation, encouragement, and gratitude.

   One smile can change the world.

2. Serve others- Spread positivity! Lend a hand to someone who needs assistance, provide something you have that someone can use, give to those in need, compliment others, share, and help one another to rise.

   "We rise by lifting others."
   Robert Ingersoll

3. Follow your faith and your Magical Breadcrumbs - Opening yourself to the magic of the Universe

connects you with Source and yourself, and together they will lead you to your passions, destiny, and life purpose.

"You have to find what sparks a light in you so that you, in your own way, can illuminate the world."
Oprah Winfrey

4. Share your divine gifts and talents- Sharing your individuality and uniqueness inspires and supports the rising of others, leading to the joy and happiness you are searching for.

   "If you want to give light to others you have to glow yourself."
   Thomas Monson

5. Love one another- In all situations, choose love. Love above fear, hate, anger, jealousy, and greed. Choosing love is always finding the positive and showing gratitude and appreciation first.

"Nothing can dim the light which shines from within."
Maya Angelou

Afterword

In early 2022, D'Ann received guidance from Source that she would be writing a book and was led almost immediately to the publisher, who would make it a reality. The purpose became apparent once she let go of the ideas her ego thought the book would be about.

The book would be called 'Magical Breadcrumbs', and the messages would serve her purpose from Source to unite women and help feminine energies rise together to lead in the emergence of the new Earth. Magical Breadcrumbs is for all the women caught in the middle of knowing there is more to life but are suppressed or trapped within limiting beliefs, preventing them from rising to their potential.

D'Ann is honored to be part of each reader's journey in discovering the magic of the Universe. She is grateful to everyone who opens their hearts and minds to new possibilities and reads her words. She asks that you conclude this reading with the following:

Source, Spirit, Universe, Divine, God or Higher Self,

I am grateful for the Magical Breadcrumbs that led me to read this book. And I thank you for quieting my mind to allow the messages and beauty of the Universe to penetrate my heart. From this day forward, please help me to remember my perfection, recognize my Magical Breadcrumbs and be fearless in following them.

Namaste

About the Author

D'Ann Marie Blatt's life only appears ordinary. After a Twin Flame encounter lit her soul on fire, she awakened spiritually and received her life purpose from Source. Now she is guided by angels, spirit guides, and all those in her highest vibration of her soul family to unite women, help others break out of limiting beliefs, rise to their divine perfection, and shine their inner lights.

With over twenty years of experience in leadership, a background in early childhood education, and a Bachelor of Arts in Business Administration, D'Ann brings a unique combination of experience, education, and passion to helping others unlock their hidden potential; D'Ann is an author, lightworker, mentor, public speaker and play facilitator.

When not writing, D'Ann meditates, spends time with her family, enjoys the sunshine, or visits a local park to bird-watch and walk Sadie, her Yorkie-Chihuahua. D'Ann lives in Las Vegas, Nevada, with her husband, two sons, and three furry children.

Follow her on social media or visit her website Magicalbreadcrumbs.com and join her in discovering breadcrumbs together. After all, Magical Breadcrumbs are not just signs and synchronicities; they are a way of life.

References

Algar, J., Armstrong, S., Hand, D., Heid, G., Roberts, B., Satterfield, P., Wright, N., Davis, A., & Geronimi, C. (1942). *Bambi* [Film]. RKO Radio Pictures.

Grimm, Jacob and Wilhelm Grimm. (1812*). "Hansel and Gretel."* Edited and translated by D.L Ashliman. Folklore and Mythology Electronic Texts, 2011.

The Holy Bible, King James Version. Cambridge Edition: 1769; *King James Bible Online*, 2023. www.kingjamesbibleonline.org.

Plato. (1993). The Symposium; and The Phaedrus: Plato's erotic dialogues. Albany :State University of New York Press.

Want More Magic?

- ✓ Be someone's Magical Breadcrumb! Purchase additional copies of this book to gift others in uncovering their Magical Breadcrumbs, and bravely shine their inner lights.
- ✓ Join the Magical Breadcrumb movement on social media:
  - ○ Use #MagicalBreadcrumbs to tag photos and videos of your Magical Breadcrumbs to raise awareness of signs and synchronicities from the Universe.
- ✓ Connect directly with D'Ann at magicalbreadcrumbs@gmail.com to:
  - ○ Share your personal connections to the book content.
  - ○ Refer contacts of people, places, and organizations that can benefit from learning about Magical Breadcrumbs.
  - ○ Recommend ways to help D'Ann fulfill her mission of assisting others in recognizing, harmonizing, and rising to align their lives with their soul's perfection.
  - ○ Collaborate on projects of awakening, conscious awareness, and Twin Flames.

✓ Visit Magicalbreadcrumbs.com to see all the new ways D'Ann is fulfilling her mission and purpose, register for upcoming events, and claim your three gifts:

1- Download the Historical Magical Breadcrumbs Journal Template
2- View a video message from D'Ann.
3- Read extended Magical Breadcrumbs content.

Acknowledgments

Stephany, thank you for being my cheerleader, supporting my journey, and while I wrote this book. I am so grateful for the Universe bringing us together, and I can't wait to see what our Magical Breadcrumbs will lead us to in the future.

Natasa, when Source directed me to write this book, I was guided to you through Magical Breadcrumbs. Thank you for encouraging me and providing the team to help me 'smash it out'!

Sabrina, you captured my true essence and inner light in my personal brand photographs and helped me overcome some blockages towards my Magical Breadcrumbs! I can't thank you enough.

Glossary

Provided to assist you in comprehending some of the content and concepts that may not be familiar to you; yet must be understood from the author's perspective.

Abundance- Unlimited high vibrational desires, defined by each person individually. Including but not limited to love, joy, happiness, health, and wealth.

Chakras- Invisible, rotating energy centers located throughout the body that can be seen and felt through intuition. To obtain optimal health and happiness each must be open and flowing as they are attached to nerve centers and organs.

Clairaudience- A miracle ability to hear messages, sounds, or voices directly from the Universe; only the intended recipient can hear the words or sounds. They bypass the ears and human hearing capabilities.

Claircognizance- A psychic ability everyone can tap into that allows for an otherwise unexplained clear knowing of something. You know and feel "It just is."

Collective- Groups of people with similarities.

Destiny- A person's ultimate life obtainment determined before this lifetime.

Divine- Perfectly created and intended by God/Spirit/Universe/Source

Ego- The portion of yourself navigating you through only this single lifetime. Ego is how you present yourself, your views, possessions, professions, etc. Often tied to money, lower vibrational energies, and is susceptible to programming and beliefs. The ego lies invisibly and creates false protections for survival. It is essential to recognize the necessity and value of the ego while consciously recognizing the ego's primary function is not necessarily in alignment with the soul's purpose. When one's bodily functions are no longer measurable, the ego dies with the human body.

Feminine energy- The energy usually associated with a woman. Lies within both men and women. Requires one to balance both energies through thoughts and actions. Like Twin Flames, those expressing excessive or unexpected feminine energy are here to teach the world free and liberated love.

Free-will- A Universal Law allowing every human to make their own choices, actions, and decisions without interference from the Universe.

Happenstance- A combination of happening and circumstance.

Heaven on Earth- Each of our perceptions of a perfect life. It is a recognition of the desires within the heart space of where your Magical Breadcrumbs can lead you.

Higher powers- God, Spirit, Universe, Source, angels, and spirit guides

Higher self- The voice of your soul. It knows what is best for you, your life's purpose, and how to live joyfully and in abundance.

Higher vibrational energy- Energy connected to all positive emotions, actions, and circumstances, including love, joy, and gratitude.

Intention- A desire of one's mind, heart, and soul. Without attachment to the result, one releases preconceived notions of how it will happen.

Karma- The cause and effect of our actions; Can be positive or negative. Thoughts, intentions, and actions in lifetimes imprint on the soul, resulting in future patterns resurfacing to reward good deeds through happiness and good fortune or provide opportunities for resolution and to make better choices.

Karmic relationships- A profound relationship to teach valuable lessons and heal karmic debts. Often turbulent and emotionally exhausting, lasting for a short duration. Essential purpose to one's healing and growth. Similar relationships will continue in life if lessons are not recognized and resolved.

Law of Attraction- Magnetic, energetic alignment drawing something together

Lower vibrational energy- Connected to all negative emotions and actions, including fear, anger, greed, jealousy, and hate.

Magical Breadcrumbs- A morsel of wisdom, a synchronicity or sign used by higher powers attempting to lead one toward their highest good and ultimate destiny. A method of communicating tidbits of guidance from the Universe.

Manifestation- The ability to achieve hopes and dreams when one's ego and soul align; one is in flow and connected to the Universe. The Law of Attraction makes manifestation possible.

Masculine energy- Usually associated with men. Lies within both men and women. Requires one to balance both energies through thoughts and actions. Those heavily weighted in ego tend to misuse this energy for power and control.

Mirror Soul- See Twin Flame

Namaste- Translation: "The divine within me bows to the same divine within you." A way to acknowledge love, kindness, and gratitude.

Personal power- An attitude and ability to choose how to act and feel. A self-confidence to make confident choices and advocate for one's beliefs, and wants, without compromising. Personal power is about consciously choosing to use inner strength and autonomy to lead one through life.

Polarities- Contradictory tendencies; extreme opposites.

Physical body- The vehicle your soul and ego are sharing in this lifetime.

Religion- Beliefs based upon denomination and often a written book of scripture, also likely involve rituals within a house of worship and expected practices. People often see one chosen religion as superior to others and those following a religion find spirituality to represent something dark, evil, and unacceptable.

Souls- The essence of who we are. Souls incarnate into a human body shared with an ego as the vehicle in this life. Souls are here to experience this life, learning, evolving, and supporting humanity over many incarnations. Souls are pure love and light, beautiful and the essence of perfection, living eternally and free throughout many lifetimes. Before awakening, the soul is often overshadowed by the ego. A soul is the part of someone you often hear about in near-death, out-of-body experiences, or paranormal activity. Souls can separate from the body and remain an energetic being. Souls are not reliant on the human body to exist, but to experience human life. They do not care about ego or worldly things. The soul is your spark.

Soul contracts- Agreements made between souls before incarnating into this life consisting of commitments, relationships, and interactions that will occur to assist another soul in this lifetime to learn lessons or direct someone toward something that is established for one's greater good during this incarnation.

Soul knowledge- A belief that cannot be traced to this lifetime and therefore is accepted as an imprint upon the soul and is transferred through the ego through claircognizance.

Soulmate- A commonly accepted relationship existing because their souls agreed to support and accompany one another in this lifetime; soulmates are part of a soul family connected for eternity.

Source- One term to address the higher power, God, Spirit, and Universe and their angel messengers.

Spirituality- Believing in a higher power but not being confined to one religion or belief. The ability to use heart resonance to choose practices and beliefs to follow. It can be seen as the gray area between the black and white.

Spiritual awakening- A sudden, profound personal transformation that reminds one of their direct connection with Source and the higher perspective and existence of a spiritual reality. Expanding thoughts and reality to infinite possibilities through extrasensory perceptions. Also referred to as spiritual ascension and spiritual enlightenment.

Twin Flame- Also known as a mirror soul. One soul sharing the exact blueprint and energetic frequency split into two entities but joined together for eternity. Very rare human connection, as they are not always incarnated on Earth simultaneously. When united in a lifetime, the purpose is aligning the ego with its soul truth, returning belief to Source, and fulfilling a divine mission agreed upon before incarnating.

Universal laws- Intrinsic laws of the Universe that do not change, including but not limited to the Law of Attraction.

Notes to Analyze

Use this space to record the emotional responses or triggers that arise from reading the book content. Behind these feelings are the keys to uncovering the shadows within you standing in your way of receiving your Magical Breadcrumbs.

Then, look for areas where you identify similarities in your entries and attempt to uncover the pattern and the hidden beliefs to implement conscious changes and evoke healing.

_____

_____

_____

_____

_____

_____

_____

_____

_____

_____

D'ANN MARIE BLATT

Author of Magical Breadcrumbs, D'Ann Marie Blatt, is on a mission to change one million lives by sharing a secret that she uncovered in her own life. After a Twin Flame encounter lit her soul on fire, and she awakened spiritually, she realized that unseen divine guidance has surrounded her the entire time. She calls these Magical Breadcrumbs.

Now, she is fulfilling her life's purpose to help others break out of limiting beliefs by following their own breadcrumbs. With over twenty years of experience in leadership, a background in early childhood education, and a Bachelor of Arts in Business Administration, D'Ann brings a unique combination of experience, education, and passion to helping others remember and rise to their divine perfection.

D'Ann's authentic nature captivates and engages audiences, leaving them looking around every corner in their lives for Magical Breadcrumbs! She is an author, lightworker, Twin Flame, mentor, public speaker, and play facilitator who presents her signature topics as keynote and interactive experiences:

Uncovering the Divinity Within

- ✓ Revealing veils of illusions
- ✓ Breaking through belief barriers
- ✓ Discovering divine magic
- ✓ Mind-blowing concepts to live by
- + Living a life led by Magical Breadcrumbs

To book D'Ann for your next event:

 Magicalbreadcrumbs@gmail.com 🌐 www.magicalbreadcrumbs.com

Printed in the USA
CPSIA information can be obtained
at www.ICGtesting.com
CBHW081415151223
2653CB00005B/15

9 781922 982902